CRITICAL ESSAYS ON

THE TEMPEST

William Shakespeare

D0321424

Editors:
Linda Cookson
Bryan Loughrey

LONGMAN
LITERATURE
GUIDES

Longman Literature Guides

Editors: Linda Cookson and Bryan Loughrey

Titles in the series:

CONTENTS

PREFACE

Like all professional groups, literary critics have developed their own specialised language. This is not necessarily a bad thing. Sometimes complex concepts can only be described in a terminology far removed from everyday speech. Academic jargon, however, creates an unnecessary barrier between the critic and the intelligent but less practised reader.

This danger is particularly acute where scholarly books and articles are re-packaged for a student audience. Critical anthologies, for example, often contain extracts from longer studies originally written for specialists. Deprived of their original context, these passages can puzzle and at times mislead. The essays in this volume, however, are all specially commissioned, self-contained works, written with the needs of students firmly in mind.

This is not to say that the contributors — all experienced critics and teachers — have in any way attempted to simplify the complexity of the issues with which they deal. On the contrary, they explore the central problems of the text from a variety of critical perspectives, reaching conclusions which are challenging and at times mutually contradictory.

They try, however, to present their arguments in a direct, accessible language and to work within the limitations of scope and length which students inevitably face. For this reason, essays are generally rather briefer than is the practice; they address quite specific topics; and, in line with examination requirements, they incorporate precise textual detail into the body of the discussion.

They offer, therefore, working examples of the kind of essay-writing skills which students themselves are expected to develop. Their diversity, however, should act as a reminder that in the field of literary studies there is no such thing as a 'model' answer. Good essays are the outcome of a creative engagement with literature, of sensitive, attentive reading and careful thought. We hope that those contained in this volume will encourage students to return to the most important starting point of all, the text itself, with renewed excitement and the determination to explore more fully their own critical responses.

How to use this volume

Obviously enough, you should start by reading the text in question. The one assumption that all the contributors make is that you are already familiar with this. It would be helpful, of course, to have read further — perhaps other works by the same author or by influential contemporaries. But we don't assume that you have yet had the opportunity to do this and any references to historical background or to other works of literature are explained.

You should, perhaps, have a few things to hand. It is always a good idea to keep a copy of the text nearby when reading critical studies. You will almost certainly want to consult it when checking the context of quotations or pausing to consider the validity of the critic's interpretation. You should also try to have access to a good dictionary, and ideally a copy of a dictionary of literary terms as well. The contributors have tried to avoid jargon and to express themselves clearly and directly. But inevitably there will be occasional words or phrases with which you are unfamiliar. Finally, we would encourage you to make notes, summarising not just the argument of each essay but also your own responses to what you have read. So keep a pencil and notebook at the ready.

Suitably equipped, the best thing to do is simply begin with whichever topic most interests you. We have deliberately organised each volume so that the essays may be read in any order. One consequence of this is that, for the sake of clarity and self-containment, there is occasionally a degree of overlap between essays. But at least you are not forced to follow one — fairly arbitrary — reading sequence.

Each essay is followed by brief 'Afterthoughts', designed to highlight points of critical interest. But remember, these are only there to remind you that it is *your* responsibility to question what you read. The essays printed here are not a series of 'model' answers to be slavishly imitated and in no way should they be regarded as anything other than a guide or stimulus for your own thinking. We hope for a critically involved response: 'That was interesting. But if *I* were tackling the topic . . .!'

Read the essays in this spirit and you'll pick up many of the skills of critical composition in the process. We have, however, tried to provide more explicit advice in 'A practical guide to essay writing'. You may find this helpful, but do not imagine it offers any magic formulas. The quality of your essays ultimately depends on the quality of your engagement with literary texts. We hope this volume spurs you on to read these with greater understanding and to explore your responses in greater depth.

A note on the text
All references are to the New Penguin Shakespeare edition of *The Tempest*, ed. Anne Righter.

Peter Reynolds

Peter Reynolds is Lecturer in Drama at the Roehampton Institute of Higher Education, and author of Text into Performance *(Penguin, 1985).*

ESSAY

The Tempest — Act I, scene 1: a dramatic analysis

In the middle of the nineteenth century, theatrical fashions on the British stage were dominated by an almost insatiable appetite for spectacle. The new technology available to theatres (notably controlled gas lighting and hydraulic machinery) provided producers with the means to create extravagant illusions. The author of *Alice in Wonderland*, Lewis Carroll, recorded in his diary a visit to the Princess Theatre in London in the summer of 1857, to see a performance of *The Tempest*. The staging of the storm and shipwreck that opens the action made a powerful impression on him:

> In the evening we visited the Princess's: the pieces were *A Game of Romps* [a one-act farce by J B Morton] and *The Tempest*. The scenic effects in *The Tempest* certainly surpass anything I ever saw there or elsewhere. The most marvellous was the shipwreck in the first scene, where (to all appearance) a real ship is heaving on huge waves, and is finally wrecked under a cliff that reaches up to the roof. The machinery that works this must

be something wonderful: the scene quite brought back to my mind the storm I saw at Whitby last year, and the vessels plunging through the harbour mouth.

But such almost cinematic realism was not possible in the Jacobean theatre. The staging of the shipwreck that began their productions of Shakespeare's *The Tempest* was a very different, but no less exciting theatrical event. Lewis Carroll was struck by the illusion of reality created in the theatre, Shakespeare's audience, although themselves not averse to the delights of spectacle, would primarily have enjoyed the storm scene that opens the play for what it contributed to the overall *meaning* of the play as a whole. Shakespeare's actors largely relied on spoken language and physical gesture rather than sophisticated technology to establish the location and significance of the action. As the chorus in Shakespeare's *Henry V* says to the audience, it is 'on your imaginary forces' that the actors must work. A modern reader likewise cannot hope to indulge in the vicarious thrills that flow from illusionistic drama of the kind described so vividly by Lewis Carroll. But, if we look with care at the opening scene as it appears on the printed page of a modern edition of the play, we too can create, using our own 'imaginary forces', a performance that lifts Shakespeare's 'storm-tossed bark' off that page and into the theatre in our minds.

[On a ship at sea]: *A tempestuous noise of thunder and lightning heard.*

These opening stage directions indicate that all the considerable energy and resources of the Jacobean stage-crew would have been called upon to make sounds which would represent a storm at sea. To do this they had a primitive but effective method of making the noise of thunder (a cannon ball rolled down a metal trough), and probably also a means of simulating a flash of lightning. On entering the stage, the players enacting the Master and Boatswain would doubtless have used their acting skills to imitate the walk of those trying to maintain balance on the deck of a moving vessel. Their costumes would have provided the audience with information about their calling and status. These impressions, established through visual text (i.e. that which is conveyed in ways other than through dialogue), are then confirmed by what is spoken — an exchange of titles reveals who the two actors represent:

MASTER Boatswain!
BOATSWAIN Here, Master.

The Master is first to speak. He alerts his second-in-command (and the audience) to the imminent danger that faces them, and gives orders to 'Speak to th'mariners'. Thus the opening minutes of the action establish the storm (through sound and lighting effects); that what is happening takes place on board a ship (through the physical gestures of the two actors); the status of those being represented (through their costumes and any gestures such as a salute that might indicate the ship's hierarchy), and the circumstances that now threaten the lives of the men on board: 'we run ourselves aground'. As the Master exits it should be noted that he is apparently relinquishing command: he has given orders and left the execution of them to the Boatswain, who is now in charge of the efforts to save the ship, its passengers and crew.

The crew now enters. The greeting of the Boatswain, 'Heigh, my hearts! cheerly, cheerly, my hearts!', perhaps indicates that the immediate task of this group of actors is to signal to the audience the understandable unease and misgivings of the crew: they look frightened. But the Boatswain encourages them with his warm greeting. His knowledge of what to do in order to combat the threat to the good order of the ship posed by the storm is reassuring. There is no uncertainty here; his orders are clear. What the audience should see in a performance is an ordered and purposeful response to the threat of chaos. Everyone onstage now knows what to do, and when and how to do it. In performance the audience needs to be given sufficient time to register this fact before the arrival of the second group of actors, those representing the court of King Alonso of Naples.

This second-group is in marked visual contrast to the first. The sailors' costumes may have been simple — possibly ragged and with bare feet, but those worn by the King and his court would have indicated not only their vastly superior material wealth and status, but also their inappropriateness for a ship at sea in a storm. But the real contrast comes because, unlike the mariners, they do not know what to do. They have no access to skills or knowledge that will fit them for a suitable, i.e. a practical, response. They are out of their element.

The actor playing the character with the highest rank is first to speak. (You should remember that much of this dialogue would almost certainly have been shouted above the noise of the storm.) As befits a king, Alonso assumes that he is, or should be, in command. He issues two instructions and asks a question:

> Good Boatswain, have care. Where's the Master? Play the men.
>
> (I.1.9–10)

His first instinct is to give an order; his second to seek for the highest available authority. He obviously finds it difficult to accept that the Boatswain is in charge of the ship, and therefore also in charge of him! Instead of getting the immediate answer his rank and position could reasonably lead him to expect, he and the rest of his company are brushed aside by the Boatswain, who issues a blunt instruction of his own: 'keep below'. Of course this is meant literally, but it can also mean in this context 'keep below me', i.e. accept that I am in charge here. One of the King's company (Antonio) won't accept this brusque command and steps in to confront the Boatswain. He repeats the King's question. The Boatswain's response is sharp and angry:

> Do you not hear him? You mar our labour. Keep your cabins! You do assist the storm.
>
> (I.1.13–14)

It indicates, in the din still presumably being kept up offstage as well as on it, that the voice of the Master can be heard, issuing commands to other groups of mariners. But the Boatswain does what on dry land would be unthinkable, and even treasonable: he *orders* the King's party to 'keep your cabins'. There is no immediate indication that they will comply. Thus, the conflicting elements to which the storm gives rise are mirrored in this, the first of many conflicts of authority chronicled in the play.

It is the 'honest old councillor', Gonzalo, who, perhaps literally, steps between Antonio and the Boatswain. He tries to calm the situation by reminding the Boatswain of his social obligations: 'remember whom thou hast aboard'. But the Boatswain is concerned with a far more fundamental issue than the observance of social conventions; he is trying to preserve the lives of all on board. He has to remind Gonzalo (and the King), of an important truth:

> If you can command these elements to silence, and work the peace of the present, we will not hand a rope more. Use your authority. If you cannot, give thanks you have lived so long...
>
> (I.1.21–24)

The authority of a king is not absolute. On this ship, threatened as it is with extinction, it is of no consequence. Here power and control are vested in the Boatswain and the crew. Other men, however exalted their rank, live their day-to-day lives in a very different environment to this, and are now simply in the way. Authority is vested in a boatswain, not a king. Gonzalo's wisdom as a councillor now asserts itself. He appears to recognise that compromise is necessary, and acquiesces with the commands of his social inferior. He sees that, rough though his manner may be, his logic is essentially correct: 'I have great comfort from this fellow'.

Whilst the Boatswain and the aristocrats have been in contention as to whose authority carries the more weight, the crew have been busy all around them. The Boatswain, when he re-enters, reaffirms his authority. He is sure and precise (and Shakespeare, as many editors of this play have subsequently remarked, was at pains to be accurate) in the orders he now issues to the crew:

> Down with the topmast! Yare! Lower, lower! Bring her to try with main-course.
>
> (I.1.34–35)

But no sooner is he seen to be controlling and managing the crew's expert response to this threat to their lives, than his authority is again challenged. The re-entry of Sebastian, Antonio and Gonzalo, signals a renewed human conflict. Unlike the King and the Prince, who had the wisdom to listen to good council and retire below, surrendering their authority (to that of the Boatswain and, ultimately, to that of God, to whom they now pray), two of these men will not accept that anyone other than themselves should exercise control of their destiny. The point being made here is that whoever commands the ship (or the ship of state which the vessel metaphorically represents) governs effectively *only* with the consent of all those on board. Antonio and Sebastian withhold that consent. Their subsequent confrontation with the Boatswain degenerates into an exchange of insults. A verbal storm erupts which, in its ferocity, almost matches that of the tempest itself:

> BOATSWAIN   Yet again! What do you here? Shall we give o'er and drown? Have you a mind to sink?
> SEBASTIAN   A pox o'your throat, you bawling, blasphemous, incharitable dog!
> BOATSWAIN   Work you, then.
> ANTONIO   Hang, cur, hang, you whoreson, insolent noise-maker. We are less afraid to be drowned than thou art.
>
> (I.1.38–44)

The famous stage direction, '*Enter Mariners wet*' signals the end of the confrontation and the beginning of the end of the scene. Until this point is reached, the ship's crew are seen to be coping with the tempest. But, after this fierce argument, there is a demonstrable sign (the wet mariners) that things have now taken a turn for the worse. The men have apparently given up hope that their own efforts can save them and, like King Alonso, they too resort to prayer. Gonzalo tries unsuccessfully to counsel Antonio and Sebastian to join them. But prayer does not appeal to them. Antonio, against *all* the evidence that the audience has witnessed, blames the crew and the Boatswain for their present predicament:

> We are merely cheated of our lives by drunkards.
> This wide-chopped rascal — would thou mightst lie drowning
> The washing of ten tides!
>
> (I.1.54–56)

The climax of the scene comes with the break-up of the ship. The printed text seems to imply the use of improvisation in perform-ance both on the part of the actors and stage-crew. The latter are now required not only to create the sound of a storm, but also a 'confused noise' within. As so often in Shakespeare, the more extreme the situation, the more simple and direct is the language used to express it. 'Mercy on us!' 'Farewell, my wife and children!' 'Farewell, brother!' These cries may well move an audience to feelings of compassion. The concluding lines are given to Gonzalo. Despite his understandable desire to be anywhere other than where he now finds himself, he is nevertheless resigned to the will of a superior authority: 'The wills above be done'.

But, of course, it is not the 'wills above' that have been done, it is the will of Prospero, as becomes clear in the next scene when the hard-pressed stage-crew take a break, and leave the work to the two actors playing Prospero and Miranda. As we noted at the beginning of this essay, Lewis Carroll was delighted and impressed by the skill of the Victorian stage-technicians in creating such a believable illusion of a shipwreck on the stage of the Princess Theatre. But the character of Miranda is also powerfully affected by an illusion. As she tearfully confesses to her father:

> O, I have suffered
> With those that I saw suffer! A brave vessel,
> Who had, no doubt, some noble creature in her,
> Dashed all to pieces. O, the cry did knock
> Against my very heart! Poor souls, they perished.
>
> (I.2.5–9)

But of course they did not perish. Miranda, like the inhabitants of the ship itself, has been deceived. It is Art, not Nature, illusion not reality, that is at work here. To reassure his daughter, Prospero must carefully explain that the evidence of her eyes is not to be trusted, the spectacle of the shipwreck was not all it appeared to be:

> The direful spectacle of the wrack, which touched
> The very virtue of compassion in thee.
> I have with such provision in mine art
> So safely ordered, that there is no soul —
> No, not so much perdition as an hair
> Betid to any creature in the vessel
> Which thou heard'st cry, which thou saw'st sink.
>
> (I.2.26–32)

Like a Victorian stage-manager, Prospero's art has created an illusion so effective that it has convinced those who saw it, as well as those caught up in it, that it was in fact real. This is only the first demonstration of Prospero's magical art. Throughout the play we see further examples of his skill as an illusionist — in the banquet scene (III.3) and the grand Masque of Ceres (IV.1). However, ultimately Prospero recognises that, in his own words, this is 'rough magic' that, once it has served its purpose, must be relinquished:

> I'll break my staff,
> Bury it certain fathoms in the earth,
> And deeper than did ever plummet sound
> I'll drown my book.

(V.1.54–57)

For, despite his power to control and manipulate events, Prospero can distinguish between illusion and reality, and ultimately he opts for the imperfections of the latter. Although Miranda marvels at what he creates, and Ferdinand is content to live forever on an island that he thinks of as Paradise (IV.1.122–124), Prospero knows that it is to the world of reality, to Milan, the real world that he once neglected for 'the bettering of my mind' (I.2.90) that they must all return.

Storms, whether illusory or real, are not uncommon in Shakespeare, famous examples being found in *Macbeth*, *Othello*, and *King Lear*. They are used not only because they generate theatrical interest and excitement, but also because storms provide powerful metaphors heralding scenes of impending disorder and dislocation in society. In *Macbeth*, for example, a storm brings with it the three 'black and midnight hags' — heralds of the chaos and confusion in Macbeth's bloody career. In *Othello*, the storm at sea encountered by the Moor in his crossing from Cyprus pre-figures the tempest of jealousy that will soon tear apart his relationship with Desdemona. In *King Lear*, the storm on the blasted heath is a vivid metaphor for the turmoil in the mind of that demented monarch. But the storm that begins this, the last great play that Shakespeare wrote, is different from the others: it is used to introduce important ideas about the constant struggle to maintain authority in the face of chaos that the subsequent action explores and develops.

The audience have witnessed in this opening scene a group of people from all classes in society reacting in different ways to the huge, and eventually overwhelming odds, thrown against them by the apparently random actions that characterise the natural world. But, as we have observed, the storm that buffets them is not simply an arbitrary act of nature but has been deliberately created and, despite the appearance of chaos, is under control. It is Prospero, the magician, God-like in his power, who shapes the destiny of all those on board. Their lives are subjected to his power although they all remain in ignorance of it.

On that 'storm-tossed bark' the Master *gives* authority to his Boatswain almost immediately. The Boatswain is then seen to use it with confidence, and the mariners to follow his leadership without question. What characterises their response to impending chaos is orderly and cooperative action under a clearly defined leader. In the opening moments of the scene, although the situation is serious, it is under control and there is no threat of imminent calamity. But, with the entry of the King and other aristocrats, authority is in dispute, and the general situation of all on board begins to deteriorate. The nobility automatically assume that they, and not the humble seamen, should be in control. Thus Alonso's first thought is to issue a totally unnecessary order. It becomes clear, however, that this is a king who listens to his councillors and is able to recognise that the authority that counts here is not his own, but that vested in the Boatswain and, ultimately, in the God to whom he prays. By contrast, the responses of Antonio and Sebastian are very different. They will not cooperate, and so rebel against rightful authority.

Unusually for an opening scene by Shakespeare, the audience are *not* told who the characters are: no one is given a name. The focus of attention is therefore on the *rank* of those on board; not on their personalities. We hear only of a Master, a Boatswain, a King and a Prince. Of the four, the one with the lowest social standing is given the greatest authority. Though the audience do not learn the names of the characters, they do learn something about them that the subsequent action of *The Tempest* will confirm. For it is not the storm itself that really matters in this drama, but how individuals react to it. It is a test in which some of them do well, others badly. The critical situation on board the vessel affords an opportunity for demonstrating the wisdom of Gonzalo, the modesty of the King and Prince, and the naked aggression of Sebastian and Antonio. The audience are left in no doubt that these two, whoever they may eventually be revealed to be, have by their response to the threat of chaos posed by the storm revealed themselves to be villains, and a real threat to the order of the ship of state.

As we have seen, the opening of this play is action-packed. It is full of noise, and the sometimes frantic movements of the actors on and off the stage. In dramatic terms it is probably among the most spectacular Shakespeare ever wrote. But, more importantly, it shows us men reacting in different ways to a crisis that tests their character; reactions that will help to shape our response to the subsequent events of this strange and eventful history.

AFTERTHOUGHTS

1

Do *you* go to the theatre to enjoy 'the illusion of reality' (paragraph one)?

2

How helpful is information about Jacobean staging traditions to your understanding of *The Tempest*? Compare Reynolds's view of these with Poole's (pages 54–55).

3

Reynolds suggests that the ship in *The Tempest* is a metaphor for the 'ship of state' (page 14). What justification can you find for this?

4

This essay raises explicitly the relationship between the 'visual text' and the printed text (page 10). Is it possible to appreciate a play by reading it?

Diana Devlin

Diana Devlin has taught extensively in schools and colleges in the UK and US, and is closely involved with the International Shakespeare Globe Centre. She has published numerous critical studies.

ESSAY

Caliban — monster, servant, king

Caliban is the son of a devil and a witch and is described as a monster by Stephano and Trinculo, but he speaks and behaves as a human character. The question therefore arises whether he is to be regarded as a fully developed man capable of moral choice with a place in the social hierarchy, as a subhuman species lacking human understanding, or as a creature of the devil. In this essay I shall argue that Caliban is depicted as a man, not a beast, and as such should be viewed in the context of the human society represented in *The Tempest*.

Our first impression of Caliban is given by Prospero in the second scene of the play. He draws a contrast for the audience between his spirit Ariel, who was too 'delicate' to withstand the 'earthy and abhorred commands' (line 273) of the 'foul witch Sycorax' (line 258) and her son, 'A freckled whelp, hag-born' (line 283). Ariel embodies the elements of air and fire and is called 'fine apparition', but Caliban is called 'earth', 'tortoise' and 'hag-seed'. It is Prospero who says that Caliban was 'got by the devil himself' (line 319), but his attitude is so clearly biased by his disgust and contempt for Caliban that we may question whether he believes this literally. Later, in IV.1, he expresses his disappointment in Caliban, condemning him as 'A devil, a born devil, on whose nature/ Nurture can never stick' (lines 188–189). As far as the functions they serve, Ariel is Prospero's 'servant', and Caliban his necessary 'slave':

> We cannot miss him. He does make our fire,
> Fetch in our wood, and serves in offices
> That profit us.

(I.2.311–313)

Caliban himself simply acknowledges Sycorax as his mother and Setebos as her god, without reference to witches or devils. We may infer from this that he views himself as a man.

Miranda also contributes to the definition of Caliban's nature. At first, she clearly considers him a man, alluding to him as a 'villain', and speaking of Ferdinand as the *third* man she saw, Prospero and Caliban being the first two. Later, however, she speaks of having known only two men. Her view of Caliban has clearly changed. In comparison with the 'brave new world' represented by Ferdinand and the other Italian courtiers, Caliban no longer seems to her worthy of the name of man.

The other characters who encounter Caliban are Trinculo and Stephano. Trinculo thinks he is either a man or a fish, but is influenced by first seeing him in the terror of the storm. Stephano, finding the confusing heap that is Caliban/Trinculo, initially thinks it is a devil or a monster. His first idea is to take him home and get money by putting him on show. But as soon as Caliban tastes the 'celestial liquor' Stephano offers him, he goes on his knees in worship. Stephano is flattered by this response and immediately agrees to let Caliban be his 'true subject' and swear allegiance like any man promising loyalty.

It seems then that Caliban is a man, but so unlike those from Italy that his humanity is ambiguous to them.

Our view of Caliban is very much influenced by knowledge of the social context in which the play was written, and is now read and performed. Although *The Tempest* is a fantasy set on an island in the Mediterranean, it has been virtually impossible for any reader or audience from Shakespeare's time onwards to dissociate the dramatic situation from the discovery of the New World and the colonisation of the Americas. From travellers' accounts of Shakespeare's time it was clear that ethnic differences, and the desire to impress, inspired half-believed stories of monsters as fantastic as all the imagined devils of medieval times, or of later science fiction. Within that context, Caliban is seen as a fish-like monster. But he also symbolises the natives of America, and of other parts of the world colonised by Europeans.

The name Caliban may have been chosen as an anagram of 'can(n)ibal', a word coined in the sixteenth century as a variation of 'Carib', an inhabitant of the West Indies. In the Names of the Actors in the first edition of *The Tempest* (printed after Shakespeare's death) Caliban is described as 'savage', the word already used for natives of the colonies. Derived from the French word for 'wild', it already carried a double connotation. Some regarded the savage as a primitive innocent, whom civilised man corrupted, while others associated the savage with cruelty and inhumanity. In particular, a French writer, Michel de Montaigne, had written an essay, 'Of Cannibals', which Shakespeare had certainly read, for he quotes from its English translation. Montaigne argued strongly that the laws and customs of American natives were not barbarous or uncivilised but were merely different from those of Europeans, and indeed that in their simple and self-sufficient way of life they recalled the 'Golden Age' which classical writers described. Yet others described savages as 'human beasts' and wrote of their brutality, treachery, ugliness and infidelity.

How does Caliban fit into this debate on savagery? In Prospero's eyes he is guilty of brutality in having tried to violate Miranda's honour; he is treacherous, betraying Prospero to Stephano; by all accounts he is ugly; but he is not unfaithful to his own god, Setebos, or to his island home.

Indeed, the island brings out the best in Caliban. Whenever he describes it, his language loses its characteristic gruffness. He says that when he loved Prospero he showed him:

> ... all the qualities o'th'isle,
> The fresh springs, brine-pits, barren place and fertile.

> (I.2.336–338)

He describes further delights to Stephano:

I prithee, let me bring thee where crabs[1] grow;
And I with my long nails will dig thee pignuts,
Show thee a jay's nest, and instruct thee how
To snare the nimble marmoset, I'll bring thee
To clust'ring filberts, and sometimes I'll get thee
Young scamels from the rock. Wilt thou go with me?

(II.2.164–169)

This has the lightness and eagerness of a young lover and would touch the hearts of listeners more sensitive than Stephano and Trinculo. But the speech that sets him most apart from these two is when they are fearful at the music of the island and he, the master of the situation for once, reassures them (III.2.136–144). It is not clear whether the music he describes is created by Prospero's magic or if it is the natural music of the island, linking it with the 'music of the spheres', which Shakespeare's contemporaries believed in as an expression of celestial harmony. Whatever its source, Caliban's receptiveness to it expresses a spirituality which raises him above base humanity.

In assessing Caliban's 'savagery' we need to remind ourselves again that the maligning of his character comes mainly from Prospero. In him Shakespeare depicts, with almost prophetic insight, the history of the white man's attitude to indigenous populations in the colonies: the change from kindness to oppression, and from the encouragement of mutual cooperation to the take-over of native territory, the temptation of alcohol, which reduces the native to a state of stupidity and dependence, and the confusion and hatred induced by the clash of different moralities.

These thoughts inevitably impinge on our understanding of *The Tempest*, and affect our response to it. But to further our understanding of the character Shakespeare has depicted, let us examine Caliban in the social context that is within the play.

The character of Caliban contributes significantly to an important social theme in *The Tempest*, that of freedom, authority and service. We learn that when Prospero first came to the island he freed Ariel from imprisonment. Caliban, perhaps born

---

[1] Crab apples rather than crabfish.

on the island and certainly bred there, had early learnt to fend for himself. Then Prospero arrived. With the mastery provided by his books, he easily took command of Caliban, who, for his part, became a willing pupil of Prospero's language. We might interpret this rudimentary education as a symbolic release from the imprisonment of ignorance. In exchange, Caliban helped Prospero and his daughter to survive on the island. However, at the time that the action of the play begins, neither Ariel nor Caliban enjoys freedom any longer. Ariel is bound by fear and gratitude to carry out Prospero's commands, while Caliban is kept a partial prisoner and plagued with aches and cramps if he does not obey his harsh master. He is much embittered. In his first speech he curses Prospero. In the second, he explains his resentment: that Prospero has usurped his rightful place on the island:

> This island's mine, by Sycorax my mother,
> Which thou tak'st from me.
>
> (I.2.331–332)

Prospero's words are ambiguous. He says that Sycorax was 'hither brought with child,/ And here was left by th'sailors' (I.2.269–270), and then speaks of the son 'that she did litter here' (I.2.282). However, we may note that Sycorax, like Prospero, had settled on the almost uninhabited island after being banished from her home, and also that she did some deed that was good enough for her to avoid the death penalty ('for one thing she did/ They would not take her life' — I.2.266–267); two points which may gain her some sympathy with the audience. Caliban then laments Prospero's change of attitude, from kindness to harshness. This change affects him much more deeply than his loss of possession. In fact the second part of this speech shows that it was not until the change that Caliban began to resent Prospero's authority:

> When thou cam'st first
> Thou strok'st me, and made much of me. . .
> . . . And then I loved thee
>
> (I.2.332–336)

He curses Prospero, not because of his position of authority, but because he has changed Caliban from a loyal, loving servant to an imprisoned slave:

> All the charms
> Of Sycorax — toads, beetles, bats light on you!
> For I am all the subjects that you have,
> Which first was mine own king; and here you sty me
> In this hard rock, whiles you do keep from me
> The rest o'th'island.

> (I.2.339–344)

It seems, then, that while Ariel aspires to be free, to fly merrily from cowslip's bell to bat's back without a care in the world, Caliban, given a free choice, would not seek total liberation but willing service.

We shall find two striking instances in the play when labour and service are willingly and joyfully undertaken. The first is when Caliban chooses to serve Stephano as his master, singing exultantly of his freedom from compulsion:

> No more dams I'll make for fish,
>   Nor fetch in firing
>   At requiring,
> Nor scrape trenchering, nor wash dish.
>   Ban, Ban, Cacaliban
>   Has a new master — get a new man!
> Freedom, high-day! high-day, freedom! Freedom, high-day,
>   freedom!

> (II.2.176–183)

However, this choice is a delusion in the eyes of Trinculo and of the audience, who can see that Caliban has simply become a slave to the bottle. The second instance follows immediately, offering a parallel. Ferdinand, compelled by Prospero to perform Caliban's menial task of bearing logs, expresses the joy of labour done with love:

> This my mean task
> Would be as heavy to me as odious, but
> The mistress which I serve quickens what's dead,
> And makes my labours pleasures.

> (III.1.4–8)

Ironically, what makes Ferdinand's task a pleasure is the very same force which destroyed Caliban's pleasure, namely his attraction towards Miranda. The sight of a handsome prince — or, as he himself fears, a young king — bearing logs before Miranda, who tries to help him, is in marked contrast to Caliban's brutish appearance and his repulsiveness to her.

Closely linked to the idea of service is that of authority and rule. How a kingdom should be ruled for the benefit of its people was a question that interested Shakespeare's contemporaries as much as it does the modern world. A self-contained community, such as is found on an inhabited island, is a theme that has inspired many writers to consider the possibility of perfect government, as Sir Thomas More did in his essay on *Utopia*. In *The Tempest*, Gonzalo, King Alonso's most loyal courtier, tries his hand at it while trying to distract his master from his grief. Imagining himself a king on the island, he weaves a fantasy round the dream of an ideal community. Ironically, the speech Shakespeare gives him (I.1.150–173) is almost a direct translation from a passage in Montaigne's essay 'Of Cannibals', already referred to, describing government among the 'savages'. Gonzalo's ideal of mankind living peacefully, happily and humanely is even more perfect than Montaigne's, excluding wars as well as laws and private property. Antonio and Sebastian ridicule Gonzalo's flight of fancy. Most pertinent to mention here is the latter's interjection when the older man says 'No sovereignty', to say 'Yet he would be king on't' (line 159). For many dreams of a perfect community are wrecked on the rock of sovereignty. How can government be perfect if it is *imposed* on the people? *The Tempest* does not present the 'savage' community described by Montaigne and imagined by Gonzalo, but focuses on the problem of authority and rule.

When Caliban was alone on the island he was simply 'mine own king'. But when he and Ariel began to serve Prospero, a reciprocal relationship was created, with Prospero governing his tiny kingdom on the island much more forcibly than he had ruled Milan. Indeed it was through lack of government that he had lost his dukedom, relinquishing the management of his state to his brother in order to pursue his own studies. (His situation might be compared with King Lear, who also abdicated authority but wished to retain the ceremony and state of kingship.) In *The Tempest* we see that kingship has no meaning without subjects who give their allegiance and service. Alonso, King of Naples, is powerless when separated from his kingdom and people, wrecked upon the island. The plot to kill Alonso is a fruitless one unless the conspirators can find the means to get back to Italy and rule there. Meanwhile, Stephano has more real authority than Antonio, Alonso, or Ferdinand, who believes himself to be king because he thinks his father drowned. For Stephano, Caliban's service is of real value on the island, and the plot against Prospero, though easily thwarted, has more practical point than the courtiers' conspiracy.

Throughout the play, Prospero manipulates his powers quite tyrannically, in order to achieve his higher purposes. It is a mark of Caliban's refinement of moral sensibility that he learns to recognise the superiority of his old master. He first becomes disillusioned with his sottish companions when they cannot discriminate, as he can, between the real source of Prospero's power, his books, and the trumpery that distracts them from seriously threatening that power. In the end he achieves a reconciliation with Prospero, even as the latter berates him, obeying his final command without hesitation:

> Ay, that I will; and I'll be wise hereafter,
> And seek for grace. What a thrice double ass
> Was I to take this drunkard for a god,
> And worship this dull fool!

(V.1.295–298)

One early Shakespearean critic regretted this change:

> I always lament that our author has not preserved his fierce and
> implacable spirit in Calyban, to the end of the play; instead of
> which, he has, I think, injudiciously put into his mouth, words
> that imply repentance and understanding.
> (Joseph Warton, 'Remarks on the Creation of Character', in D J
> Palmer (ed.), *The Tempest* — Macmillan Casebook, 1968)

Certainly it seems that Caliban has enlarged his idea of willing service. Henceforth he will be more careful to evaluate the object of his allegiance. The phrase 'seek for grace' has a specifically Christian association which suggests that he has sensed something greater than a human master to aspire towards serving.

But what is to become of him after this? At the end of the play, Prospero has reconciled himself to the brother who usurped his dukedom, restored Ferdinand to his father the King, successfully arranged the young man's marriage to his daughter and freed his servant Ariel. The royal party prepares to return to Milan, all ends neatly tied. Except one. No mention is made of Caliban. Does he depart with the others to Milan, risking the humiliating 'shows' the lesser characters see him fit for? Or does he too have his rightful rule restored, remaining as king on a now totally uninhabited island? That is preferable, but such a possibility adds a sad twist to the theme of ruler and subject, for in the character of Caliban we see illustrated the beginning of social awareness, the first gropings towards an understanding of relationship.

There are other Shakespearean 'happy' endings, where one character stands apart from the general mirth; Malvolio, who, at the end of *Twelfth Night* threatens revenge; Jaques in *As You Like It*, who chooses voluntary exile instead of returning to the court with the other characters. We should perhaps see, at the end of a production of *The Tempest*, the figure of Caliban abandoned by Prospero, isolated from the mood of harmony and relief of those who return to Milan, forced to remain in a world he has now learnt to recognise as lonely and loveless.

AFTERTHOUGHTS

1

What do you understand to be the distinction between 'servant' and 'slave', as argued in this essay? Do you agree with Devlin's claim that Caliban has changed 'from a loyal, loving servant to an imprisoned slave' (pages 24–25)?

2

How helpful is it to think of the play as a study in colonisation (pages 21–23)?

3

Do you agree that Prospero uses his power 'tyrannically' (page 27)?

4

What do you assume becomes of Caliban at the end of the play? And how useful do you find it to speculate on this?

Christopher Hardman

Christopher Hardman lectures in English at Reading University, and is the author of numerous critical studies.

ESSAY

Dramatic pattern and expectation in *The Tempest*

In this essay I want to examine aspects of the dramatic form of *The Tempest*, paying special attention to some examples of the way in which Shakespeare exploits his audience's recognition of allusions to, and adaptations of, contemporary dramatic practice and ideas about drama.

My first example shows how Shakespeare used a fairly well known definition of the difference between comedy and tragedy, actualising a metaphor it provided in the setting of his play. The tempestuous opening, and the promise of 'calm seas' and 'auspicious gales' at the end (V.1.315) of *The Tempest*, may seem to be there simply to cause the shipwreck and to assure the audience that the voyage back to Italy will be safe, while at the same time echoing at first the disturbed passions and then the harmonies of the action. However, they also reflect a definition

---

¹ The essay *De Tragoedia et Comedia* (Concerning Tragedy and Comedy) by two fourth-century writers, Evanthius and Donatus, was frequently printed as an introduction to Renaissance editions of the works of the Roman dramatist Terence set for study in Grammar Schools. For a general account of the contents of the essay see M Doran, *Endeavors of Art: A study of form in Elizabethan Drama* (Madison, Wisconsin, 1954), pp.105ff.

of dramatic form which was read by Elizabethan Grammar School boys in one of their school text books.[1] Comedy, it was said, began with turbulence and ended with calm, while the reverse was true of tragedy. In *The Tempest* the suggestion of metaphor in this description is dramatically realised in the events of the play itself.

No other play by Shakespeare has such a strikingly exciting and naturalistic opening as *The Tempest*. A storm rages at sea and a ship carrying a king and his court is torn apart. The scene would certainly have tested the technical resources of the Jacobean theatre, as it often does those of the modern theatre. It is quite clear that the storm is meant to seem real and natural. These mariners are 'wet', and the air is full of shouted instructions which are meant to seem like the real language of sailors struggling to save the ship. Shipwrecks are common in romantic stories and plays, where they characteristically give rise to wonder rather than belief. It is, however, not quite what one would expect in a play following classical models of construction, as *The Tempest* seems to be. Yet paradoxically, while making this typically romantic feature seem real, Shakespeare may at the same time be seen as presenting a dramatic demonstration of Sir Philip Sidney's classically based advice to playwrights in his *Defence of Poesie*.[2] The audience is indeed, as Sidney advises, thrust into the middle of the action, and Shakespeare begins with 'the principal point of that one action which [he] will represent'. The alternative, to have presented the events in chronological order, beginning in Milan before Prospero was usurped, and following the account given in the extended retrospective narration taking up so much of the second scene, would have been condemned by Sidney as following the manner of the historian rather than the dramatic poet. His *Apology* contains a clearly disapproving description of such a method:[3]

> '. . . two young Princes fall in love. After many traverses she is got with child, delivered of a faire boy, he is lost, groweth a man,

---

[2] The quotations from Sidney are all taken from the edition of *An Apology for Poetry* edited by Geoffrey Shepherd (London, 1965), pp.134–135.

[3] This sounds rather like Shakespeare's attempt to handle events spread over an extended period of time in *The Winter's Tale*, the play which he wrote immediately before *The Tempest*.

falls in love, and is ready to get another child, and all this in
two hours' space . . .'

(p.134)

To the mind of the Renaissance classicist, 'the stage should
. . . present but one place, and . . . both by Aristotle's precept,
and common reason, but one day' (p.134), rather than starting
with the birth of the major characters and presenting the events
of many years; and accordingly, the location of the play is
restricted to the island, during a period of about three hours. So
the surprising beginning of *The Tempest* not only marks a new
attempt at naturalism based on incredible romantic material,
presenting a sense of the real in a daring theatrical spectacle,
but also combines it, at the same time, with a new adoption of
classical structure, which strives for naturalism of a different sort
in the presentation of time and space.

Of course, just before this structure becomes completely
obvious, when Prospero himself recounts things done at a former
time and in another place, the audience learns with Miranda
that the storm was the product of Prospero's art.

> The direful spectacle of the wrack, which touched
> The very virtue of compassion in thee,
> I have with such provision in mine art
> So safely ordered, that there is no soul —
> No, not so much perdition as an hair
> Betid to any creature in the vessel
> Which thou heard'st cry, which thou sawst sink.

(I.2.26–32)

The terrible and disturbing effects of the first scene are negated
once we are aware that they are to be attributed to magic. The
method establishes comic expectations almost from the start.[4]

There is no hint in the first scene that there is anything

---

[4] As the second scene proceeded, a member of the audience who had seen
Shakespeare's previous play *The Winter's Tale* only a few months earlier,
might well have recognised that he was on familiar ground. Two people, a
father and child, standing on the shore and talking about a shipwreck in a way
which changes the audience's reaction to what has happened, was how the
second, comic part of the tragi-comedy began in *The Winter's Tale*. There,
truly terrible events were described in such a way that a humorous response
was nevertheless called for from the audience.

magical about any of it, and no production should ever let the audience guess that there is from the way it is staged. The shock of discovery is intentional and disorientating. We can no longer be sure about anything in the play, no longer distinguish for certain between art and reality. It is a confusion shared by everyone within the play except Prospero. At the end of the play the uncertainty seems to spill over into the world of the audience. Prospero appears before us, not as the actor who has played the part, but as a character of fiction needing the assistance of the real audience to complete the voyage back to a fictional Milan. The sense that art is able to change things in a fashion impossible in real life is apparent here: Prospero's art is at work within the play as is Shakespeare's in constructing it, for this kind of thing only happens in fiction.

One of the distinctions Aristotle made between comedy and tragedy was that the plots of the latter should either be drawn from history, or at least give the impression that they were true, while the plots of comedies were allowed to be more obviously fictitious. At the beginning of *The Tempest* the move seems to be from a world of kings, courtiers, real storms and shipwrecks and — though we do not know it immediately — of political manipulation, dynastic marriages and treachery, to a world set apart, full of illusions, and patently fictitious. Yet the real world is never forgotten. Prospero's island is certainly not idyllic, for here the events of that real world are replayed, but the environment is obviously a controlled one. Interestingly we do not find out the truth about the 'men of sin' wrecked there until the controlled context is established, and this naturally influences our expectations: we do not expect their wicked plans to succeed in this comic environment. However, to take what happens in the last scene of *The Tempest* to be the conventional, stereotype comic ending characterised by harmony and happiness does not seem entirely convincing to everyone. Gonzalo, characteristically, sees the outcome as providential:

> Look down, you gods,
> And on this couple drop a blessèd crown!
> For it is you that have chalked forth the way
> Which brought us hither.

(V.1.201–204)

He asks rhetorically:

> Was Milan thrust from Milan that his issue
> Should become kings of Naples? O, rejoice
> Beyond a common joy, and set it down
> With gold on lasting pillars. In one voyage
> Did Claribel her husband find at Tunis
> And Ferdinand her brother found a wife
> Where he himself was lost; Prospero his dukedom
> In a poor isle, and all of us ourselves
> When no man was his own.
>
> (V.1.201–213)

Here Gonzalo is very clearly interpreting events with hindsight. One does not elsewhere get the impression that divine providence has brought them to the island, nor that Prospero's usurping was all for the best. Some critics see here a harmonious comic vision in which the errors of the past are put right. Art can provide the second chance which life does not. A wiser Prospero is restored and the succession, so important politically, is secured now that Ferdinand and Miranda are to marry. But the coupling of this union with that of Claribel far away in Tunis, as events worthy of inscribing on pillars of gold, should not make us forget Sebastian's account of the opposition to Claribel's marriage and her own reluctant obedience to her father (II.1.125–133), which Gonzalo then admitted was the painful truth. Gonzalo's attempt to remake the play as an example of a fortunate fall, to look forward with optimism and without recrimination or bitterness, simply does not truly reflect the events. We are not sure, for example, what to make of the silence of Antonio and Sebastian. If they are unregenerate, as it seems they may be, there might be an ominous touch to the circularity of the action: Gonzalo's vision presupposes that men will change; if they do not, history has a habit of repeating itself. Prospero's forgiveness of his brother's faults is prefaced by a recognition that there can be no prospect of brotherly reconciliation between them, although it would have been quite easy for Shakespeare to have brought them together in open reconciliation, as he indeed did with brothers in similar circumstances in *As You Like It*. That he decided not to do so here should warn us not to be satisfied with such comic optimism as Gonzalo's.

This last scene opens out into the political world of Milan and Naples, back towards the world of the storm, the 'real' world where we began. In this play that world appears only in a scene of sixty lines, in the recollection of Prospero, and of course in the attempts of those who are shipwrecked to import its murderous opportunistic values to the island. In the 'real' world Prospero's success cannot be quite what it is on the island. Without his magical powers predatory enemies will be more dangerous. Time is carefully calculated and constantly observed by Prospero, yet it is a time apart, very different from time in the 'real' world. The declaration that 'Every third thought shall be my grave' (V.1.312) is a perfectly proper sentiment for a noble Christian man, who should always be aware of his mortality, and live each day conscious that it might be his last, and it certainly does not mean that Prospero is necessarily expecting death to be imminent; yet it does remind the audience of the transitory nature of the world of Milan and Naples, and the world in which the audience itself lives. It has been suggested that Prospero's political success is limited, for the dynastic marriage so carefully arranged will eventually result in Naples absorbing Milan, merely taking a stage further what Antonio's homage to Alonso has already begun. Yet this ignores the dilemma of a duke without a son, and with a daughter who, though virtuous, is unschooled in the ways of the political world and needs protection. Milan deserves a worthy ruler, Prospero a worthy heir, and Miranda a worthy husband. Antonio could have been none of these, whereas the testing of Ferdinand on the island suggests that he can be all of them. The young couple seem to offer the best future for both Naples and Milan. We are asked here to consider both the demands of political reality and the rewarding of moral worth which accords with our normal expectations of the conclusion of a comedy.

The audience's consciousness of the dangers that lie in wait in the world of Italian politics is sharpened by Miranda's wonder at the appearance of Alonso and his court:

> Oh wonder!
> How many goodly creatures are there here!
> How beauteous mankind is! Oh brave new world,
> That has such people in't!

As Prospero wryly remarks:

> 'Tis new to thee.

(V.1.181–184)

Of course they are from a world new to someone who has lived her life on an island peopled only by her father and the spirits and monsters at his command, and may seem beauteous to her; but we know that their fair outsides may be deceptive. Her wonder signals the customary revelations and reunions to be expected at the end of a romantic comedy, while Prospero's realistic remark — for he knows these men of old — limits that expectation.

Finally I want to look at *The Tempest*'s relation to two other branches of contemporary theatre, first to point out the alternative path the action might have taken into revenge tragedy, a path which would have been very familiar to Shakespeare's contemporaries, and an awareness of which is important in understanding the play; and then to examine briefly some aspects of a topic which has in general been exhaustively treated many times elsewhere: the relationship between the play and the masque.

The Jacobean audience of *The Tempest* would have been acutely aware that here was a story which could easily have been treated in a different way. *The Tempest* is to some extent defined by the play which Shakespeare chose not to write. It exists against the background of a contemporary dramatic tradition of plays characterised by intrigue and revenge. The most likely treatment for material dealing with Italian politics, usurpation, murders, family divisions, loyalty, infidelity and love, would have seemed to Shakespeare's contemporaries to have been a tragedy of intrigue and revenge, and there were plenty of examples and models ready to hand, many of them appropriately Italianate. In *The Tempest* the potential for developing further intrigue is considerable. Sebastian and Antonio conspire against Alonso and prepare to murder the King and the faithful Gonzalo while they sleep, continuing to behave on the island in the opportunistic and unscrupulous way in which they behave in the world outside. Caliban, Stephano and Trinculo attempt to repeat the conspiracy against Prospero which exiled him from Milan so long ago, intending to kill him, take possession of the island, and make Miranda Stephano's queen. Of course Prospero's control thwarts both noble and vulgar conspiracies, and the ludicrous nature of the latter cannot be taken very seriously. Yet we can recognise the outlines of the plotting to be found in tragedies of intrigue and revenge, and compare the treatment afforded it here by comparison with the mayhem common in those fictional worlds where plots, counter-plots and stratagems are so rife that revengers become enmeshed and cannot perform straightforward acts of revenge, and where unmitigated, merciless revenge may be pursued at the expense of guilty and innocent alike.

The most notable and influential play in this sub-genre of intrigue and revenge is *The Spanish Tragedy*. There the stage action takes place within a frame presided over by a personifi-cation of Revenge accompanied by the ghost of the nobleman Andrea, eager to witness revenge taken on 'the author of [his] death'. Shakespeare's Prospero also views the events which discomfort his old enemies and seeks to encourage repentance in them, played out before him as in some kind of performance, one which he directs from the start. In *The Spanish Tragedy* the action comes completely under the direction of the revenger, Hieronimo, in the denouement, when revenge is effected under cover of a play staged at court. Prospero's direction throughout also involves the employment of dramatic set-pieces, but none of these leads to a bloody conclusion like Hieronimo's play, for Prospero eschews vengeance, though 'struck to the quick' by the 'high wrongs' of his enemies. How far Prospero's intentions are obvious before the beginning of Act V when, after the develop-ment of the relationship between Ferdinand and Miranda, we certainly do not expect a thoroughgoing revenge ending; and whether his response to Ariel's sympathetic reaction to the cour-tiers' plight represents a sudden abandoning of a planned revenge upon them all has often been debated. Some have considered that at least the possibility of a 'mixed' ending, that is one in which the wicked are punished and the virtuous saved, remains right up to the exchange with Ariel. In the formal organisation of the play's action it is certainly this exchange which initiates the comic catastrophe, and at the same time ensures that an audience is conscious that an alternative course was possible.

Prospero's dramatic set-pieces are arranged to conclude each section of the action of *The Tempest*: the banquet and the harpies, the betrothal masque, and the pursuit of Caliban and his cronies by spirits in the shape of dogs. In this he has frequently been compared to a masque presenter arranging 'entertainments'. Jacobean masques celebrated and praised monarchs, and sometimes offered them counsel about good kingship. The first part of the performance came to comprise an anti-masque, in which the antithesis of the courtly ideal, a world of vice and disorder was presented, and this was then replaced by dancers figuring an ideal virtuous world which reached out to include the courtly audience in its celebratory dancing. The illusory banquet that is conjured up and then snatched away by Ariel appearing like a harpy (III.3) may be thought to serve as an anti-masque to the betrothal masque (IV.1), the voluptuous temptation of the banquet contrasting with the control of the passions required of the lovers; but it is strikingly different from what one might expect of an anti-masque in a number of respects. Though the scene is presented before a king, he is a shipwrecked king with the remnants of his court, and they find themselves not just watching, but incorporated in an anti-masque in which they have been cast in the role of vices to be expelled. The counsel it offers Alonso is of an unusually outspoken kind, openly castigating royal misdeeds. The betrothal masque too is unusual in that it is presented as contrived by the ruler whose family betrothal it celebrates, and may thus be seen to be a powerful and personal expression of Prospero's own ideal world, rather than that of a poet employed to praise him; but Prospero is suddenly recalled from the vision by the thought of Caliban's 'foul conspiracy'. An audience does not take the threat from Caliban and his cronies seriously, and rightly so, but it is none the less true that the most ludicrous and inefficient of conspirators can succeed if the victim is asleep, as even Caliban knows. The unfinished masque and Prospero's turning from the vision of a wished-for ideal reminds us of the initial occasion so many years before when, 'rapt in secret studies' (I.2.77), he failed to be awake to his brother's intentions. The kind of idealising represented by Prospero's enactment of his 'present fancies' in the betrothal masque can involve a neglect of worldly ends (I.2.89) as dangerous for a prince as being shut up in a library 'bettering' his mind.

Such a modification of masque material serves to supplement and reinforce those other elements in the play which prevent the audience from taking a naïve and unthinking view of the harmony of the conclusion. In the case of each dramatic type I have been considering: masque, intrigue-and-revenge play, and romantic comedy, Shakespeare disturbs the audience's normal expectations. What we discover in *The Tempest* is defined by our awareness of what might have happened — dramatically speaking — and did not, as well as by what we have witnessed on the stage.

AFTERTHOUGHTS

1

What distinctions are drawn in this essay between comedy and tragedy?

2

What are the two different sorts of 'naturalism' that Hardman has in mind on page 32?

3

Hardman says that 'no production should ever let the audience guess' that the storm at the beginning is illusory (pages 32–33). Do you agree with him?

4

Do you agree that *The Tempest* is a 'comedy'?

William Tydeman

William Tydeman lectures in English at the University College of Wales at Bangor, and is author of a number of critical studies.

ESSAY

Act I, scene 2: Prospero's tale?

For many readers and playgoers the chief barrier to their enjoyment of *The Tempest* is undoubtedly its second scene. Immediately upon our first entry into Prospero's enchanted kingdom it rears up like a forbiddingly prolonged mountain-range which we are forced to cross if we are to reach the sweet meadows beyond. Act I, scene 2 is not the longest single scene in Shakespeare — that dubious distinction is held by the immensely lengthy scene which concludes *Love's Labour's Lost* — but it is certainly his longest scene of exposition in which necessary information is transmitted to the audience in order to enhance their understanding of the ensuing action.

Length alone does not account for the deadening effect this scene so often has on stage and in the study. It is not exactly that nothing happens: we are introduced in sequence to five of the leading characters. And in Ferdinand, who enters the action at line 374 and encounters Miranda a few lines later, is foreshadowed the eventual reconciliation of the old unregenerate world of Europe with the brave new moral realm inhabited by Prospero. By the close the plot is moving: Miranda is infatuated with the Neapolitan prince, and her father has used his magic to take him prisoner. But what many find hard to endure, whether reading in the library or watching from the stalls, is firstly the seemingly excessive time taken by Prospero in recounting to an auditor whose interest appears fitful —

PROSPERO   Thou attend'st not!
MIRANDA   O, good sir, I do

(I.2.87–88)

— the events leading to a situation whereby those responsible for ejecting him from Milan are even now about to be brought to book for their act of usurpation. Furthermore, having engaged in a protracted explanation of his presence on the island, Prospero proceeds to lavish a further duologue on Ariel, during which he finds it needful to remind the airy spirit of its origins, its unhappy experience in the cloven pine, and his own magnanimity in releasing his servant from torment, all of which Ariel might be expected to be familiar with. Lastly, Caliban must be hauled forth for interview, and space again devoted to recalling the savage's former status, his abuse of his master's trust, and the reasons for his present role as dogsbody to Miranda and her father. It might reasonably be asked why, to put the audience in the picture, Shakespeare should have employed so blatantly obvious a dramatic device as informing characters of matters which they might fairly be assumed to know pretty well already! The presentation of Miranda as eager to learn her antecedents might be exempted from this charge, but in the scenes with both Ariel and Caliban, Shakespeare clearly obliges the characters to tell each other not what *they*, but what their *audiences*, require to be told!

To the apparent clumsiness of the exposition of one of Shakespeare's last dramatic efforts we shall clearly need to return, since the impression of ineptitude may prove only superficial. However, most people's dissatisfaction with the scene goes further than merely voicing a complaint about the seemingly primitive technique utilised to put us in possession of the relevant facts. We may well feel that the structure of the first part of the scene up to the encounter between Ferdinand and Miranda is singularly unenterprising, consisting as it does of three separate duologues between Prospero and one other character, the only break in this pattern in the course of nearly 400 lines coming with Miranda's interjection at line 352 charging Caliban with ingratitude. Even here a number of editors including Dryden and Theobald have sought to assign this speech to Prospero, no doubt on the grounds that the words:

> I pitied thee,
> Took pains to make thee speak, taught thee each hour
> One thing or other. When thou didst not, savage,
> Know thine own meaning, but wouldst gabble like
> A thing most brutish, I endowed thy purposes
> With words that made them known
>
> (I.2.353–358)

sound more appropriate in Prospero's mouth than in that of the teenaged Miranda. But the emendation deprives us of the touching image of the precocious child teaching the inarticulate native, as well as cancelling the effect of a momentary respite from Prospero's remorseless narration.

And this must surely be the third main stricture about the entire scene, that it is dominated throughout by the protagonist in such a way that he reduces all the supporting characters to subordinates of himself. For example, there is no reason to doubt that Shakespeare portrays Prospero as a loving and devoted father, and yet his frequent sharp enquiries in the early part of the scene as to Miranda's interest in his tale can easily make him seem tetchy and demanding, and later her ardent advocacy of Ferdinand's trustworthiness receives from her parent a series of crushing snubs:

> MIRANDA Make not too rash a trial of him, for
> He's gentle, and not fearful. [nobly born and no coward]
> PROSPERO   What, I say,
> My foot my tutor? Put thy sword up, traitor . . .
>
> MIRANDA   Beseech you, father!
> PROSPERO Hence! hang not on my garments.
> MIRANDA   Sir, have pity.
> I'll be his surety.
> PROSPERO   Silence! One word more
> Shall make me chide thee, if not hate thee. What,
> An advocate for an impostor? hush!
>
> (I.2.468–470; 474–478)

Perhaps this is not to be taken more seriously than any fairy-tale-like 'test', of which Ferdinand's later imprisonment and forced labour at the log-pile are further instances, and we should not over-emphasise the role of Prospero as heavy father. Yet as Anne Righter shrewdly points out in her Introduction to the New Penguin edition of the play, the relationship with Miranda is a curiously flawed one, which contrasts the anguish of Prospero's recollected pain with his daughter's innocent inability to share or fully respond to it:

> Essentially, she is bewildered by this story which sets out to enlighten her but is continually changing direction as Prospero forgets about or abruptly remembers her presence.... [His] continual nagging at Miranda in the course of the narration, his anxiety lest she fail to comprehend, emphasizes the distance between father and daughter, the difficulty of communication. And indeed, it will hardly appear subsequently that Miranda has taken in what her father had to tell her. When she first meets Ferdinand, later in the same scene, the prince makes perfectly clear whose son he is. Yet Miranda not only shows no sign of connecting him with the story she has just heard, she seems genuinely perplexed by Prospero's unfriendliness. Never once in her scenes with Ferdinand does she refer to the events of the past or the share which Naples had in them.
>
> (pp.10–11)

Perhaps Miranda's attention did wander, despite her protestations to the contrary, but her father's pent-up vengeful anger has excluded her rather than drawn her closer to him. Although she represents a spirit of loving gentleness which he eventually embraces, at this stage in the action he is as insulated from the benign influence of his 'cherubin' as he is from the other figures whom he dominates and manipulates. His role is to command, and in Act I, scene 2 he is introduced exercising that uncompromising function.

How can we come to terms with these formidable stumbling-blocks? There are many questions to resolve and issues to explore before we can assimilate into the texture of *The Tempest* what appear to be the artistic and dramatic limitations of the exposition scene. Some decades ago when it was fashionable to denigrate Shakespeare's last plays or romances as the work of a tired, disillusioned, cynical playwright content to pen potboilers to please a public willing to swallow any kind of sentimental story from his hands, the alleged weaknesses and oddities of the second scene of the play might have been dismissed as examples of indifference on the part of a writer who no longer cared about his art. But the vigour and richness of the language, the multiple levels of response to their content, have reinstated the final plays as anything but trite or facile: it seems clear that while Shakespeare's genius moved into a new phase when the King's Men acquired the indoor playhouse at Blackfriars in 1608–1609, this only focused his energies on satisfying the growing vogue for more sophisticated, less 'realistic' dramas than the open-air playhouses were accustomed to provide. Whatever lay behind Shakespeare's decision to treat the exposition scene in *The Tempest* as he did, it was not because he was bored with or cynical towards the demands of his clientele.

The success of the play must depend in part on our knowledge of incidents prior to the opening episode of shipwreck and potential disaster, and there were only two principal methods of informing an audience of what had happened: one was to include the depiction of such events as part of the stage action, the other was to provide an account of what had taken place, either in the dialogue itself, or through the use of a choric narrator. In *The Winter's Tale* Shakespeare had chosen to dramatise both the quarrel and estrangement of the two kings, Leontes and Polixenes, and their ultimate reconciliation, along with Leontes's recovery of his wife and daughter, both presumed dead. To connect the two phases of his narrative, spanning almost sixteen years, he had recourse to the figure of 'Time, the Chorus' to magic away the intervening period, so that the dark jealousies of winter and the fresh blossoms of spring could form contrasting panels of one diptych.

In *The Tempest*, however, Shakespeare prefers to make us take the past context on trust rather than witness it for ourselves. This reduction in the play's time-span certainly increases dramatic concentration, and has the incidental advantage for Shakespeare of not mirroring the structural organisation of his earlier success, *The Winter's Tale*. But the price is Act I, scene 2, and this suggests that some other motive lies behind the way in which information is conveyed to spectators on this particular occasion.

It might be argued that in none of his plays is Shakespeare ever excessively concerned to get the facts across to an audience in a very convincing or subtle manner. He is not always careful to disguise the sleight of hand by which he conveys information. Few openings could be more blatant than that of *As You Like It*, where Orlando pitches in to inform the aged retainer who has known his circumstances all his life that:

> As I remember, Adam, it was upon this fashion bequeathed me by will but poor a thousand crowns, and, as thou sayest, charged my brother upon his blessing, to breed me well: and there begins my sadness. My brother Jaques he keeps at school and report speaks goldenly of his profit: for my part, he keeps me rustically at home . . .
>
> (I.1.1–8)

To all of which and more old Adam might be forgiven for replying, 'Does he really, sir? Well now, you *do* surprise me.'

But Prospero's discourse on the circumstances leading up to the shipwreck in his territorial waters is something other than a single sketch of a basic dramatic situation: he tells Miranda of his former life in precise detail; he constantly checks to see that his narrative is not being ignored; he impresses on her his ability to control events now his enemies are within reach. To devote *so much* space to this matter and to alert Miranda, the spectators' proxy on stage, to its vital importance, indicates that Shakespeare is anything but casual about this mode of exposition, that he wishes to focus attention on Prospero in *this* role before any other.

It would have been relatively easy, had he so desired, to have conveyed all the necessary data about the connivance of Antonio and Alonso at the time of Prospero's deposition and the methods by which his removal was effected, far more convincingly and dramatically in the course of a conversation between any of the consenting parties — between say Gonzalo and his master, or between Antonio and Sebastian (which, after all, is very nearly what happens in Act II, scene 1 while the rest of the court lies asleep). His own narrow escape from death by drowning might have caused Gonzalo to muse on Prospero's presumed watery grave, or the apparent loss of

Ferdinand might have prompted Alonso to reflect with Antonio on their former crime. Shakespeare was not compelled to have Prospero himself reveal his past as he does unless there were some good reason for it.

The text offers us at least one important explanation as to why it is Prospero who recounts his own adventures. His initial tone is that of the traditional story-teller stimulating expectancy in his auditors:

> The hour's now come
> The very minute bids thee ope thine ear.
> Obey, and be attentive.

(I.2.36–38)

On two occasions his narrative is designated as a tale, once by Miranda:

> Your tale, sir, would cure deafness.

(I.2.106)

And once when he himself acknowledges the legitimacy of one of her queries:

> My tale provokes that question.

(I.2.140)

At line 137 Prospero employs the term 'story' to allude to his account. Thus the wronged Duke of Milan first assumes command of the stage as the self-appointed narrator of his own history. Not only does this increase the vividness of his description and present us with the graphic nature of his wrongs, but it also makes our initial impression of Prospero not that of a magician, nor of a duke nor a 'master of a full poor cell' but of the teller of a strange and (to Miranda) baffling story.

The significance of this transcends the mere necessity for that story to be told. Shakespeare's hero stands forth at the start of the play as the archetypal story-teller, assembling the ingredients of his tale from a variety of sources: he has his beautiful daughter ready to fall in love; he literally conjures up the handsome young prince, a trio of villains ripe for punishment at the hands of their former victim, and pairs of incongruous servants (Caliban and Ariel, Trinculo and Stepheno) to be attached to each faction. Prospero, with the fiction-writer's freedom, draws these elements together and mixes them, linking Ferdinand and Miranda, tempting Sebastian and Antonio into unholy alliance, allowing Caliban to conspire with Trinculo and Stephano, dealing gently with Gonzalo and more harshly with his old enemies (even though he finally pardons them). Prospero, like a film-director, selects events and figures to create the overall pattern he desires, rather like his prototype the Duke in *Measure for Measure*, who manipulates the inhabitants of Vienna for his and ultimately their benefit. So Prospero engineers a happy outcome for the lovers, restoring Alonso's son to his penitent father and ensuring a general reconciliation and a safe passage home. His role as creator of satisfying narratives may explain his slightly off-putting authority, the way he can make others do his bidding — sending Miranda to sleep, forcing Ariel and Caliban and other 'weak masters' to serve him, binding Ferdinand's spirits up 'as in a dream', overcoming his foes. His language too is that of the creative artist, moulding his material to support his aesthetic aims: how often we hear from Prospero's lips indications of his mastery over his human medium:

> Thou art inclined to sleep. 'Tis a good dullness,
> And give it way: I know thou canst not choose.
>
> (I.2.185–186)

> If thou neglect'st, or dost unwillingly
> What I command, I'll rack thee with old cramps
>
> (I.2.368–369)

> Come on, obey!
> Thy nerves are in their infancy again,
> And have no vigour in them.
>
> (I.2.484–486)

> My high charms work,
> And these, mine enemies, are all knit up
> In their distractions. They now are in my power
>
> (III.3.89–91)

Prospero's powers mirror those of the creative writer, the storyteller of tradition.

Once we perceive Prospero's sway over people and events,

his control over the main lines of the narrative, it seems inevitable that the action of *The Tempest* should always be presented from his point of view. It becomes a tale of injustice and retaliation, validated in the victim's own terms, so that the existence of other viewpoints is largely lost sight of, a factor which has often troubled radicals who see in Prospero's 'colonisation' of the island a faint foreshadowing of the Spirit of Empire and the White Man's Burden. Caliban's protest that his island has been annexed through an act of imperialist aggression may contain an element of truth, but the narration being firmly in the hands of the empire-builder, we are apt to lose sight of such arguments as support Caliban's contention.

Similarly, there is the original act of violence which bereft Prospero of his ducal rights and banished him to the island. Again, it is from Prospero himself that we learn of the treachery of Antonio, and the narrator clearly sees himself as more sinned against than sinning; yet it is hard for even the lawful duke to disguise the fact that he neglected his dukedom for his studies, and acted with some irresponsibility in placing too much power in the wrong hands. Instead guilt is diverted to Antonio:

> I, thus neglecting worldly ends, all dedicated
> To closeness and the bettering of my mind
> With that which, but by being so retired,
> O'er-prized all popular rate, in my false brother
> Awaked an evil nature . . .

> (I.2.89–93)

Prospero somewhat blandly excuses himself from any taint of weakness in facilitating his brother's *coup d'état*, but if he were not the story-teller, might we not be inclined to see him as an over-trusting, complacent, somewhat gullible ruler? (After all, he nearly succumbs to another assassination attempt at the hands of Caliban and his new-found friends in Act IV, scene 1.) But legitimate criticism is undermined, and Prospero is able to present himself as the hero of his own downfall.

By this method of presentation Shakespeare is in danger of minimising the complexity — political and moral — of the materials forming the substance of the play. *The Tempest* sometimes appears to offer us Prospero's vision of the universe not as it is but as he would have it to be; it is a piece of wish-fulfilment for a hero-figure whose magic powers — those of the story-teller — enable him to bring his enemies to their knees. The action of the piece is in one sense Prospero's dream of achieving his deepest desires, but in a play in which allusions to dreams abound, one might suggest that Prospero's vision of vengeance is one of those insubstantial pageants which will ultimately fade and leave not a rack behind. 'Prospero's revenge' in the end turns out to be no more than a dream-vision, and he on waking from it may (like Caliban) cry to dream again.

This is the ultimate irony of Prospero's story-telling role. In Act I, scene 2 everything seems under control, every figure seems bound to do his bidding, he knows what he wants. But as every artist knows, in the final analysis the creator does not have absolute mastery over the figments of his imagination. Nobody can really control anybody else. Anne Righter's comment on Miranda's independent spirit in failing to identify with her father's humiliation has already been quoted. Prospero proves not to be omniscient or omnipotent in the final analysis. Just as a writer cannot subdue all human life to his artistic purposes, just as an author may claim that his creations developed 'wills of their own', so Prospero has ultimately to compromise with his cherished vision and sacrifice his intended vengeance to the appeal of Ariel that he should forgive his enemies. (V.1.17–24). The climax originally intended for his story has to be abandoned.

The raw stuff of life is not to be utterly tamed. True, he has the joy of seeing the love of Miranda and Ferdinand uniting their fathers after the long bitterness; he relishes the restoration of his rights. But like Ariel, the recalcitrant spirit cannot be permanently chained down; it must be given its liberty. Caliban can never be redeemed from his bestial nature; Antonio can never be truly repentant. Prospero has lavished kindness and forgiveness on creatures who either cannot respond or who prefer freedom to serving even the most loving of masters. The close of *The Tempest* may place the accent on harmony and renewal, but the Ariels, Calibans and Antonios remain outside the charmed circle and Prospero's powers cannot prevail against them. Finally he must accept that even a brave new world contains envy, deceit, treachery, ingratitude, thirst for personal independence. By the close, the master story-teller has to acknowledge that there are limitations to his no longer sovereign powers.

AFTERTHOUGHTS

1

Did *you* feel uncomfortable with I.2, before Tydeman pointed out its potential problems?

2

What implications does Tydeman see in Prospero's use of the word 'story' at line 137 (page 47)?

3

Does Prospero 'nearly succumb' (page 49) to the 'assassination attempt' in IV.1?

4

If Prospero is an artist, is he always in control of his creations?

Roger Poole

Roger Poole has taught English in a variety of educational establishments, and is the author of numerous critical studies.

ESSAY

Music in *The Tempest*

It has often been said that *The Tempest* is the most musical of Shakespeare's plays, not merely because of the sheer quantity of its songs and music, but because music is integral to the play's performance.

The Elizabethans inherited the medieval conception of music as a symbol of divine harmony as we can see from Lorenzo's famous lines in *The Merchant of Venice*:

> Look how the floor of heaven
> Is thick inlaid with patens of bright gold.
> There's not the smallest orb which thou beholdest
> But in his motion like an angel sings,
> Still quiring to the young-eyed cherubins;
> Such harmony is in immortal souls

(V.1.58–63)

Shakespeare's contemporary, Sir John Davies, in his poem 'Orchestra: a poem of dancing' (1596), makes large claims for dancing as a pattern of the order which prevails in heaven, and dancing, which is, of course, allied to music, also plays a part in *The Tempest*.

Some ninety years later we can still find in Dryden's 'A Song for St Cecilia's Day' (1687), the same ideas:

From Harmony, from heav'nly Harmony
   This universal Frame began;
When Nature underneath a heap
   Of jarring Atomes lay,
And cou'd not heave her Head,
The tuneful Voice was heard from high,
   Arise, ye more than dead.
Then cold and hot and moist and dry
   In order to their Stations leap,
   And MUSICK'S pow'r obey.
From Harmony, from heavenly Harmony
   This universal Frame began:
   From Harmony to Harmony
Through all the Compass of the Notes it ran,
The Diapason closing full in Man.
What Passion cannot MUSICK raise and quell?

I have quoted from Dryden at some little length since what he has to say conveniently sets forth the climate in which Shakespeare wrote, and it is interesting to observe that Dryden employs the word 'diapason', meaning a whole octave, a harmony, a full volume of various sounds in concord.

We also see that in Shakespeare's *Troilus and Cressida*, Ulysses, in his speech on degree, uses a metaphor drawn from music:

Take but degree away, untune that string,
And hark what discord follows!

(I.3.109–110)

This is apt because, as with *Troilus and Cressida* and other plays, *The Tempest* is concerned with the need for due form and order lest unbridled individualism hold sway, injure the rights of others and distort the body politic.

By the Jacobean period, the masque, originating in primitive seasonal festivals, had developed into a high art form with dancing, acting, mime, music, stage architecture and elaborate stage effects, and the office of Master of the Revels established.

The Tempest was almost certainly first put on at the Blackfriars Theatre by Shakespeare's company of the King's Men in the spring or early summer of 1611. It afforded more scope for effects than the company's other house, the Globe, and generally catered for a higher class of audience. It was put on again later that year on 1 November before King James and his court in the impressive surroundings of the old Banqueting House in Whitehall, a building of considerable distinction and size. It had a stage 40 feet square and 3 feet high and a proscenium arch with the audience sitting directly in front, and was, in effect, a typical late seventeenth or eighteenth century theatre, broadly of the kind commonly found today.

In *Shakespeare's 'Tempest' as originally produced at Court* (Shakespeare Associates; London, 1920), Ernest Law comments that:

> it must have afforded full scope for scenic illusion and the presentation of 'tableaux' on a scale and in a setting of unprecedented splendour. It was thus in every way suitable for the presentation of such a play as *The Tempest*, with its frequent spectacular effects — storms with thunder and lightning and rain, spirit appearances and 'monstrous shapes', phantom banquets, 'marvellous sweet music'.
>
> (p.6)

He also comments that one important element in the performance at Whitehall was the 'Musick-Howse' by the stage, in which were stationed the King's band of some thirty or forty musicians and he records that the Revel's accounts for that year (1611):

> noted a special provision of 'a curtain of silk for the Musick House at Whitehall' — silk because, while effectively screening the musicians and singers from view, it would have offered but little obstruction to those strains of magic melody, heard by Ferdinand as it crept by him 'upon the waters', and afterwards above him: 'those sounds and sweet airs that give delight and hurt not', those 'thousand twangling instruments' that, humming about the slumbering ears of Caliban, made him — when waking — but 'cry to dream again'.
>
> (p.17)

This arrangement would certainly be right for *The Tempest* where so much of the music emerges as a surrounding impression, a spiritual presence, and we recall the wondering reactions of the various castaways:

> Where should this music be? I'th'air or th'earth?

> (I.2.388)

One of the most significant of the songs is the first one where Ariel's music allays the tempest. All on the wrecked ship have been deposited in various parts of the island, abstracted from their true selves in a dream that will become an awakening.

Ariel, working in obedience to Prospero's will, uses the heavenly power of music to lure the visitors onwards, to bring them eventually to Prospero's cell where recognition is to take place and judgement made.

In the guise of a water nymph, Ariel meets Ferdinand where he is sitting disconsolate. Ferdinand hears the invisible Ariel singing his song of invitation — 'Come unto these yellow sands . . .' (I.2.375–387) — recognises it as beautiful and responds. He is drawn forward and seeks to follow it.

Till now the storm has raged, but in this first song Ariel orders his fellow spirits to curtsy and kiss the wild waves into silence. Here we can notice the formal politeness of 'curtsied' (and 'curtsy' is a variant of 'courtesy' and 'courteous'), and the dancing imagery in 'Foot it featly', the last word meaning both 'nimbly' and 'elegantly' (see also II.2.277–278: 'And look how well my garments sit upon me,/ Much feater than before').

Ferdinand comments wonderingly on the change:

> This music crept by me upon the waters,
> Allaying both their fury and my passion
> With its sweet air. Hence I have followed it,
> Or it hath drawn me rather.

> (I.2.392–395)

The music begins to assuage Ferdinand's grief for the father he believes to be dead, while the sound of the cock and the watch-dog indicate that a kind of normality is returning, for these are sounds of everyday life swimming into his consciousness.

The words of the song can be considered as the 'libretto' to a masque dance through which the wild waves of the storm and the wild waves of sorrow in Ferdinand's heart are stilled, just as its innocent loveliness leads him towards the innocent and lovely Miranda.

Next, the solemn elegiac beauty of the second song ('Full fathom five thy father lies . . .'), with the water spirits singing their melancholy knell for the (presumed) dead Alonso, continues the washing away of Ferdinand's anguish by impressing upon him that his father, though reportedly dead, is undergoing a process of change into the rare beauty of another existence.

It also introduces a main theme of the play: that it is only through suffering and a death of the old ways that rebirth is experienced. Alonso, having undergone the physical torment of wind and wave, must now undergo the torment of conscience so that he may be transmuted through 'a sea-change/ Into something rich and strange' (I.2.401–402).

When the two lovers meet, the music, as Prospero acknowledges, produces the miracle of love at first sight and a mutual recognition of divinity:

MIRANDA   I might call him
  A thing divine, for nothing natural
  I ever saw so noble.
PROSPERO (*aside*)   It goes on, I see,
  As my soul prompts it. — Spirit, fine spirit, I'll free thee
  Within two days for this!
FERDINAND   Most sure the goddess
  On whom these airs attend!

(I.2.418–423)

Yet Prospero will allow no easy passage for Ferdinand. He has to endure and cherish before he can possess. Ferdinand, like Alonso, has to suffer (and Miranda as well, by her compassion) by accepting hard labour and hard words.

Some critics have queried Prospero's stern warnings to Ferdinand to respect the chastity of Miranda (IV.1.13–23), warnings which are repeated yet again in the admonitions in the masque which follows, but they fall in naturally with the play's insistence upon order and ceremony. The Idea of the Good is all-demanding.

Prospero is only too aware of the forces of disorder for him to find acceptable anything less than self-control and conformity. We may suppose that he recognises in Caliban the darkness of the natural man that is in himself and which he has had to subdue in the pursuit of higher things, for Prospero is representative of Renaissance man who was conscious of himself as something above the brute but lower than the angels, aspiring towards the latter but fearful of falling towards the former.

This uneasy position goes some way to account for Prospero's treatment of Caliban over and above that of anger and discipline, and for his nervous insistence on abstemious control in Ferdinand. Subconsciously Prospero fears that his own and mankind's upward aspirations may be thwarted if control is not kept of the libido, and the play certainly gives us examples in Antonio and Sebastian, and in Caliban, Stephano and Trinculo, of what licence can produce.

When Alonso, Antonio, Sebastian, Gonzalo and others find themselves cast up on another part of the island, we quickly discover the callousness and cynicism of Antonio and Sebastian, first in their offhand mocking of Gonzalo and second in their ruthless determination to kill Gonzalo and Antonio.

When Ariel enters playing solemn music, Gonzalo quickly falls asleep, as does Alonso after a little while. These two are capable of response (and sleep is a sign of innocence), but the conscienceless Antonio and Sebastian are untouched. Engrossed in their self-interest, they discuss their plans for murder.

However, just as their swords are poised to strike, Ariel's singing awakens the receptive Gonzalo, and also protects the guilty but grieving Alonso. Through music, Prospero is opening for Alonso the door of forgiveness, through which he may pass to a better life.

A little later, music interrupts when Alonso and Sebastian are again preparing an attempt at the double murder. Prospero intervenes through the device of an illusory banquet, accompanied by strange and solemn music, and with shapes which dance about it making gentle salutations and beckoning the company to participate. Shakespeare is here presenting an awesome event in which the four are to be tested. The gentle behaviour of the shapes, their dance, and the solemnity of the music offer an invitation.

The responses are significant. Alonso and Gonzalo are

deeply moved, Gonzalo remarking with more prescience than he realises:

> For certes, these are people of the island —
> Who, though they are of monstrous shape, yet note,
> Their manners are more gentle, kind, than of
> Our human generation you shall find
> Many, nay, almost any
>
> (III.3.31–35)

However, the unreceptive Antonio and Sebastian take refuge in scorn and disbelief.

As if in contempt of their attitude, Ariel — in the shape of a harpy — removes the banquet with a clap of his wings as thunder and lightning sounds.

Ariel then speaks as a messenger of vengeance, sternly rebuking the three. His tremendous speech can be taken as one of the two climaxes in the play (the other being Prospero's renunciation of his powers in V.1), and it echoes in the imagination as a denunciation on the Day of Judgement.

Ariel's words, spoken in measured tones of ringing grandeur, pierce the barrier between dream and actuality. Their condition is put starkly before them and they are told that unless they seek forgiveness, no grace can be expected. When Ariel vanishes, the shapes reappear to the accompaniment of soft music (perhaps suggesting hope) but also dealing out warning menaces and grimaces. Finally they remove the table upon which the banquet was laid.

At the end of Ariel's devastating address, Alonso's conscience is roused to such a state of despair that he acknowledges his guilt in a powerful metaphor in which the concept of musical harmony unites with the concept of divine harmony. It is for Alonso a moment of overwhelming illumination, and he understands that the natural order and the divine moral order are one:

> O, it is monstrous, monstrous!
> Methought the billows spoke, and told me of it;
> The winds did *sing* it to me; and the thunder,
> That deep and dreadful *organ-pipe*, pronounced
> The name of Prosper: it did *bass* my trespass.

Therefore my son i'th'ooze is bedded, and
I'll seek him deeper than e'er plummet *sounded*,
And with him there lie mudded.

(III.3.97–104 — author's italics)

In contrast to Alonso's guilt-stricken suicidal despair, Antonio and Sebastian make the only reaction they know: they draw their swords brazenly and uselessly, and it is to be observed that only Antonio and Sebastian, the veneered sophisticates, are irredeemable. In them, civilisation has only case-hardened their selfishness.

Discord in man is parallelled by discord in heaven. Antonio, Sebastian and Alonso have all sinned and the gods are angry. Sin is not merely some politic matter but an offence against the moral order of the universe. We know that at the end, all has been a dream: there has been no storm, no wreck, no drownings, yet, through the force of the story, we are able to see ourselves reacting to the terror of truth in the world as it might be.

When we first encounter Caliban, he enters cursing, but almost immediately we meet one of the issues in the play. Caliban arouses sympathy by recalling for the audience Prospero's initial gentle treatment of him ('When thou cam'st first,/ Thou strok'st me, and made much of me', I.2.332–333) but immediately the effect of this is weakened or nullifed when we learn of his attempted rape of Miranda. Shakespeare is thus presenting us with the eternal conflict of flesh and spirit. Brute instincts cannot be ignored, but can they be integrated into a reformed nature?

Later we see that Prospero is able to forgive his human enemies but the case with Caliban is different since he represents a species of sub-human creation, a piece of irreducible base metal; yet, for all that, he seems to have buried within him a kind of potential, and he shows more acumen, albeit in a bad cause, than either Stephano, a loud, self-seeking braggart, or Trinculo, a petty clown. The carnality and irresponsibility of the trio stand in sheer contrast to the governance of the soul which Prospero's regime seeks to establish. For Caliban, the irony of it is that he has put himself in thrall to a pair of fools, and in exchanging Prospero for these two has yoked himself to the lowest type of man.

Their vulgar songs are a far remove from the harmonies of Ariel and his fellow spirits, and even Stephano calls one of the tunes 'scurvy' (I.2.43), while Caliban himself sings mere doggerel (II.2.176–184). Quite simply, the three represent the forces of unreason.

Later, when their plans are laid to ravish Miranda, murder Prospero and make themselves lords of the island, befuddled by drink and quarrelsome, they show themselves unable to sing even a 'catch' — simple part-song — so that Ariel humorously interrupts to play the tune for them. Quietly, through his music, Ariel now takes charge, and their native disharmony and ineffectiveness is compounded as the music of his pipe and tabour lead them further astray till, after a miserable journey through brambles, mire and horse piss, they are finally hounded by dogs in what can be regarded as an anti-masque, and corralled out of harm's way in a line-grove.

Despite Caliban's behaviour, he would seem to be less guilty than Antonio, whose will perverts his actions just as his appetites control his will:

> . . . the bestial man has no sense of right and wrong, and therefore sees no difference between good and evil. His state is less guilty but more hopeless that those of incontinence and malice, since he cannot be improved.
>
> (J E Hankins, 'Caliban the Bestial Man', in *PMLA* LXII — 1947)

It seems to me that there is at least a possibility that Caliban's final words indicate that he is at the start of a process of recovery. He has lived through an experience, and has discovered the worthlessness of the two sots, Stephano and Trinculo, and is ready to sue for pardon. Prospero, who earlier (IV.1.188–189) had called Caliban 'A devil, a born devil, on whose nature/ Nurture can never stick', has also been through an experience, and now is able to acknowledge that there is something of Caliban in him: 'This thing of darkness I/ Acknowledge mine' (V.1.275–276).

We must also bear in mind the remarkable lines when Caliban tells us of his own private visions of beauty. The words — 'Be not afeard; the isle is full of noises' etc. (III.2.136ff) — are unforgettable in their loveliness, and I take them as a glimpse of an instinct for betterment.

Caliban's response here fits everything we have met in the play about the power of music, and would seem to be the later Shakespeare's reforming and revitalising of what he had written in *The Merchant of Venice*:

> For do but note a wild and wanton herd
> Or race of youthful and unhandled colts
> Fetching mad bounds, bellowing and neighing loud,
> Which is the hot condition of their blood,
> If they but hear perchance a trumpet sound,
> Or any air of music touch their ears,
> You shall perceive them make a mutual stand,
> Their savage eyes turned to a modest gaze
> By the sweet power of music.

(V.1.71–79)

We can also regard the music Caliban hears as representing in this respect a challenge to the attitude found in Plato. His idea, common enough in Shakespeare's day, is that 'There's nothing ill can dwell in such a temple' (I.2.458), i.e. that inward excellence is allied with outward excellence and vice versa.

Plato was concerned, in his *Republic* with this idea, and he considered that it was part of the task of education to bring youth into contact with the right kinds of music and poetry.

> Thus, then, excellence of form and content in discourse and musical expression and rhythm, and grace of form and movement, all depend on goodness of nature, by which I mean, not the foolish simplicity sometimes called by courtesy 'good nature', but a nature in which goodness of character has been well and truly established.
>
> (F M Cornford (trans.), *The Republic of Plato*, Book III
400C–403C (Oxford, 1941), p.87)

> We would not have our Guardians grow up among
> representations of moral deformity, as in some foul pasture
> where, day after day, feeding on every poisonous weed they
> would, little by little, gather insensibly a mass of corruption in
> their very souls.
>
> (Ibid., p.88)

Yet, in *The Tempest* we have, in Caliban, just such a moral deformity, 'a salvage and deformed slave', one who has demonstrated his unworthiness for education:

> ... on whom my pains,
> Humanely taken, all, all lost, quite lost.
> And as with age his body uglier grows,
> So his mind cankers.

(IV.1.189–192)

Ironically, it is Antonio and Sebastian, those products of high civilisation, whom music cannot touch.

When, in the betrothal masque, Prospero produces his vision of the new world, it looks back to the mythical harmonious Golden Age, but, more importantly, it looks forward to a new Golden Age when, as in the past, the joining of hands of the human and mortal reapers with the spiritual and nonmortal nymphs, symbolises, as does the music, that man should work with, and not against, the gods, and that true happiness is attained when man follows the highest good.

The formal betrothal masque forms the display centre to the drama because it offers an epiphany of the heavenly beauty and harmony to which the play has been addressing itself. Earlier, Prospero had bestowed his blessing on Ferdinand and Miranda:

> Fair encounter
> Of two most rare affections. Heavens rain grace
> On that which breeds between 'em.

(III.1.74–76)

But this is not enough, for it needs the formal reinforcement of ceremony.

The betrothal masque, with its images of beauty and fruition, gives public sanction to the high estate of marriage. It presupposes an over-arching social order counterpointed by heavenly ritual and harmony and, if we in the late twentieth century do not accept heaven quite so readily, then it is open for us to translate it into more human, or humanistic, terms.

Yet, all is not well. The breaking off of the masque to the accompaniment of a strange, hollow and confused noise suggests that the new world is not with us yet. The masque is, as Ferdinand comments, 'a most majestic vision, and/ Harmonious charmingly' (IV.1.118–119), but charms cannot solve the world's evils.

One can imagine Prospero watching the presentation with feelings of satisfaction until a vision of evil breaks in upon him as he realises in a flash of insight that all is not well. He sees, in his mind, the dark picture of conspiracy and it is no wonder that Miranda exclaims:

> Never till this day
> Saw I him touched with anger, so distempered.
>
> (IV.1.144–145)

At this critical point, what Prospero sees leaves him staggering beneath the weight of the destiny it is his to order and, in the transcendental revels speech to which this shock gives rise, Prospero seems to view life against the background of unimaginable time. As Prospero speaks, huge images of dissolution — of the masque, of life — sweep across his mind and leave him struggling with his enormous knowledge.

Ultimately, he has to abandon all magic, all charms, for truth cannot be compelled.

The working out of Prospero's plans for retribution brings all the castaways within his power. It is at this climactic point, when Ariel reports that all Prospero's commands have been fulfilled, and when he confesses that, if he were human, he would feel sorry for them, that Prospero makes his momentous decision to forgive. The desire for revenge gives way to compassion:

> Though with their high wrongs I am struck to th'quick,
> Yet with my nobler reason 'gainst my fury
> Do I take part. The rarer action is
> In virtue than in vengeance.
>
> (V.1.25–28)

This first part of his great renunciation speech ends with his commitment, his act of faith, his spiritual disarming:

> Go release them, Ariel.
> My charms I'll break, their senses I'll restore,
> And they shall be themselves.
>
> (V.1.30–32)

This deliberately taken defenceless position then becomes the starting point for the marvellous declaration which concludes the renunciation:

> Ye elves of hills, brooks, standing lakes, and groves . . .
>
> (V.1.33ff)

At the end of this affirmation, this second climax to the play when the Mage has abandoned his magic (which is, after all, in the greater context, merely 'rough magic'), Prospero calls for heavenly music as Gonzales, Antonio, Sebastian, Alonso and others stand within his charmed circle, awaiting sentence:

> A solemn air, and the best comforter
> To an unsettled fancy, cure thy brains,
> Now useless, boiled within thy skull. There stand,
> For you are spell-stopped.
>
> (V.1.58–61)

Slowly the charm dissolves like muddied waters clearing, the music probably lasting as long as the spell lasts. Functionally it provides a denouement, filling out the magical atmosphere, but symbolically it portrays the harmony that is now being restored. Prospero has chosen to relinquish magic, and what we are now witnessing are its final workings out; Ferdinand and Miranda have each other; Alonso has regained his son and found his soul; and it is given to the holy Gonzalo to pronounce the disposition of providence:

> I have inly wept,
> Or should have spoke ere this. Look down, you gods,
> And on this couple drop a blessed crown!
> For it is you that have chalked forth the way
> Which brought us hither.
>
> (V.1.200–204)

Yet Shakespeare is reminding us that there can be no complete Golden Age. Prospero's magic has forced Antonio to give back the dukedom he had seized, but the disharmonious nature of his soul and Sebastian's keeps them beyond the reach of music and rebirth. Antonio and Sebastian, more than Caliban, are the real things of darkness.

Ariel, too, must receive his promised release, and this is

part of Prospero's new future for, as Wilfrid Mellors points out in *Harmonious Meeting* (London, 1965): 'There is a fallacy — and a deficiency in self-knowledge — in Prospero's freeing of Ariel from the pine only to make a slave of him' (p.169).

We can appreciate, now that harmony has been restored after the tempest, that Ariel's final song, before he executes Prospero's last few orders, is a paean of joy for his deliverance:

> Where the bee sucks, there suck I,
> In a cowslip's bell I lie;
> There I couch when owls do cry.
> On a bat's back I do fly
> After summer merrily.
> Merrily, merrily shall I live now,
> Under the blossom that hangs on the bough.

$$(V.1.98-104)$$

Finally, all return to the freedom of the reasonable world, some changed, some unchanged, leaving Caliban master of his island, free to hear again its sounds and sweet airs, and leaving Ariel free to enter his kingdom of the elements, so long longed for.

AFTERTHOUGHTS

1

What do you learn from the opening pages of this essay about the significance of music in Elizabethan and Jacobean society? How does this affect your reading or experience of *The Tempest*?

2

How helpful is the information about Jacobean staging traditions to your understanding of *The Tempest*? Compare Poole's view of these with Reynolds's.

3

What is the relationship between the music of *The Tempest* and the play's concerns with poetry, sleep and dreams?

4

Do you agree with Poole's conclusion that all the characters return to freedom of a kind at the end of the play?

Richard Adams

*Richard Adams is Professor of English
at the Californian State University of
Sacramento, and the author of
numerous critical studies.*

ESSAY

The Tempest and the theme of social organisation

About halfway into Act II, scene 1 of *The Tempest*, the 'noble
Neapolitan', Gonzalo, seeks to divert his grief-stricken master,
the King of Naples, with an account of the sort of social organisation he would seek to impose if he were to be given government of the island on which the King's party has been cast by
Prospero's magic storm. If he were to have 'plantation' of the
place — that is, be responsible for its colonising — and to be its
king, Gonzalo declares, he would depart radically from traditional structures of government. Trade would be excluded; there
would be no need for a judicial system nor one for a system of
learning. Under his rule, extremes of wealth and poverty would
disappear and no man or woman would be obliged to serve
another. He would do away with 'Contract, succession,/ Bourn,
bound of land, tilth, vineyard' as well as the 'use of metal, corn,
or wine, or oil'. There would be no need for anyone to work:

> No occupation; all men idle, all,
> And women too, but innocent and pure.
> No sovereignty

(II.1.157–159)

All this would be possible because nature would produce everything needful in abundance and of her own accord. Accordingly, greed and discord would never take root among the people and 'Treason, felony,/ Sword, pike, knife, gun, or need of any engine' would be entirely superfluous. And over all this, Gonzalo would himself govern in such a way that it would 'excel the Golden Age'.

This rather muddled utopian vision, closely modelled by Shakespeare on lines from Montaigne's 'Des Cannibales' (Of Cannibals), is derided by the cynics in the party — Antonio and Sebastian — and is entirely ignored by the King himself. Nevertheless, it is a valuable reminder to us of the enormous importance placed by Shakespeare's contemporaries on matters of social organisation in general and on questions of order and degree in particular.

The play's opening is remarkable not only for the way in which it conveys the terrifying impact of the tempest through the words and actions of its various human victims, but also because it establishes from the start the fact that social organisation depends, to some degree at least, on setting and circumstances. In the teeth of the storm, with the ship in imminent peril of foundering, the fact that there is a king aboard is of little consequence. At such a moment, it is the Master who wields actual authority, and, under him, the Boatswain. It is the latter who orders the passengers below, not only for their own safety, but also because their presence on deck is conducive to disorder. 'You do assist the storm,' he tells them, adding, in words that shock Gonzalo into protest, his opinion that under present circumstances Alonso's title and dignity are meaningless:

What cares these roarers for the name of king?

(I.1.16–17)

Such an opening prepares us for the fact that, in *The Tempest*, we are about to see a play in which order and authority are not fixed absolutely, but shift with time and place. Indeed, in the very next scene, Shakespeare establishes the fact that, within his island domain, authority lies with Prospero and him alone, and that the King and his party, for all their noble pretensions, are entirely under his control. The idea of the island setting comes, no doubt, from the playwright's sources, from the so-called 'Bermuda Pamphlets' and stories of the grounding of the *Sea-Adventure*. But it is a particularly appropriate setting for a play about social organisation and the workings of authority.

Islands — especially small ones — have always been objects of fascination for mankind. Nowadays, we 'get away from it all' to the Channel Islands, the Canaries, the Balearics or the islands of the Aegean, with their remoteness from the buzz of city life, their comfortable quaintness and the fact that — thanks to the relative narrowness of their confines — they have the appeal of manageability. For us, islands mean the different and, perhaps, the exotic — places with which we can feel at one. (We detect something of this feeling in the initial appreciation of Prospero's island voiced by Adrian and Gonzalo in Act II, scene 1 of *The Tempest*.) But islands are not always viewed as friendly objects. If we are stranded on them alone or with just a handful of companions, they may challenge our self-confidence, our self-reliance and our ingenuity, as witness the experiences of Robinson Crusoe and those of the central characters of such novels as Ballantyne's *Coral Island* and Golding's *Lord of the Flies*. In particular, they may challenge our ability to create a viable social order, even on the smallest scale. If already inhabited, they may — as in Swift's *Gulliver's Travels* — give us the opportunity to examine the ways of alternative societies and perhaps to question some of our own values. (Once again, we can trace some of these features in the experiences of the various characters that find themselves on Prospero's island.)

It is scarcely surprising that, having in the past been the victim of usurpation and chance, Prospero should, by the beginning of the play's action, have established a firm order in his new domain. No longer sovereign duke of a city-state, his rule is essentially domestic and extends over his daughter Miranda, his slave Caliban, and Ariel and the other 'meaner' spirits of the island over whom, by means of his magic powers, he exercises control. Though he demonstrates love and concern, at various times and to varying degrees, for them all, he is a strict father and hard master who will tolerate no challenge to his authority. In the course of Act I, scene 2, when the time arrives for Miranda to hear at last the story of their joint sufferings, he insists on her noting every detail and becomes plainly irritated when her attention appears to be dwindling. When, clinging to her father's robes, she pleads with Prospero to deal leniently with Ferdinand, he rounds on her with the warning:

> Silence! one word more
> Shall make me chide thee, if not hate thee.
>
> (I.2.476–477)

But he reveals a few moments later that the attraction the two youngsters feel for each other is part of his own wider plan. Later in the same scene, Caliban reminds us that Prospero's attitude to him was at one time kindly —

> When thou cam'st first,
> Thou strok'st me, and made much of me
>
> (I.2.332–333)

— and that his affection was reciprocated. It was Caliban's infringement of the social order in attempting to rape Miranda which brought this relationship to an end and relegated him to the role of household drudge.

Ariel, though first among the spirits of the island, is also Prospero's servant and part of his domestic retinue. His service — though he acknowledges his gratitude to his master for rescuing him from the twelve-year imprisonment in a cloven pine to which he had been condemned by the witch Sycorax — is not free. At the least hint of rebellion or questioning of Prospero's intentions, he is upbraided and reminded of his former torments:

> If thou more murmur'st, I will rend an oak,
> And peg thee in his knotty entrails, till
> Thou hast howled away twelve winters.
>
> (I.2.294–296)

Nothing is allowed to disturb the order of things which Prospero has established. Just as Miranda learns of her father's past sufferings only when the appointed time for revelation arrives, so Ariel must wait patiently for the fore-ordained day of his release.

Of course, the domestic order on Prospero's island is but a shadow of the political order at the head of which he once stood as Duke of Milan ('Through all the signories,' he asserts, 'it was the first'), and the action of *The Tempest* is taken up with his efforts to win back what he has lost and to punish those who dispossessed him. There can be little doubt, however, that Prospero is himself in part responsible for the predicament in which he now finds himself. He admits to Miranda that he 'grew stranger' to the duties and cares of state, preferring instead to devote himself to the secret study of his magic arts and thus affording his 'false brother', Antonio, and 'inveterate' enemy, Alonso, the opportunity to supplant him. In the eyes of Shakespeare's contemporaries, usurpation of this kind was a crime against God, an upsetting on the grandest scale of the proper order of things, bound to have the direst consequences for its perpetrators.

Ironically, even though by the end of the play he is in a position to confront his former antagonists and to extract an admission of guilt from at least one of them, Prospero is by no means safe from the workings of intrigue — albeit on the comic level — in his acquired domain. Claiming that his master has cheated him of the island, Caliban urges the drunken Stephano to murder Prospero:

> . . . as I told thee, 'tis a custom with him
> I'th'afternoon to sleep. There thou mayst brain him,
> Having first seized his books; or with a log
> Batter his skull, or paunch him with a stake,
> Or cut his weasand with thy knife

(III.2.88–92)

— and to assume sovereign power himself. To Caliban, such a course of action constitutes not so much usurpation as revenge, since, in assuming lordship of the island, Prospero was taking what was not his in the first place. 'This island's mine, by Sycorax my mother,' he protests on the occasion of his first appearance in the play, while Prospero gives his own version of the story a few lines earlier as part of his catechising of Ariel. This 'foul witch' had formerly lived in Argier (Algiers) but had been banished from that city on account of the 'mischiefs manifold, and sorceries terrible' that she had performed there. Brought to the island by sailors, and abandoned there, she gave birth to Caliban, 'a freckled whelp hag-born' to whom possession of the island passed at her death. Comic and incompetent though it may be, Prospero takes:

> . . . that foul conspiracy
> Of the beast Caliban and his confederates

(IV.1.139–140)

against his life seriously, having the miscreants hunted down and punished cruelly:

> Go, charge my goblins that they grind their joints
> With dry convulsions, shorten up their sinews
> With aged cramps, and more pinch-spotted make them
> Than pard or cat o'mountain.

(IV.1.259–262)

Considering his past experiences, Prospero has every right to be sensitive to the dangers of usurpation. That the subject is much on his mind is borne out by his feigned accusation, in Act I, scene 2, that Ferdinand has come to his island as a spy, 'to win it/ From me, the lord on't'. And, of course, he is fully aware of the mischief being hatched by Antonio and Sebastian.

Shakespeare makes the hopeless bunglings of Caliban and his new-found friends in their attempt to overthrow Prospero a source of comic relief. There is, however, no hint of humour in the plotting of Antonio and Sebastian. We know something of Antonio's past reputation from what Prospero says to Miranda in Act I.

Presented with the opportunity to execute 'th'outward face of royalty' by his too-trusting brother's preoccupation with his own 'secret studies', Antonio became ambitious for real power. His first step was to divert the loyalty of Prospero's followers to himself:

> . . . new created
> The creatures that were mine . . . or changed 'em,
> Or else new formed 'em . . .

(I.2.81–83)

— setting 'all hearts i'th'state/ To what tune pleased his ear'. By slow degrees, Prospero lost control of his dukedom, while Antonio grew in power to the point that he felt ready to become 'absolute Milan'. However, he needed outside support to ensure the success of his coup, and turned for it to Prospero's old enemy, the King of Naples. But the price for Alonso's cooperation was a dear one: Milan, a sovereign state proud of its own independence, was to become the vassal of Naples, with Antonio, the new duke, paying Alonso annual tribute, doing him homage, subjecting 'his coronet to his crown'. Thus, in upsetting the political order within his own state, Antonio had also upset that which existed in the relationship between Milan and its neighbours. He and Alonso had even gone so far as to consider killing Prospero, but feared to 'set/ A mark so bloody on the business' on account of the strong love which the Milanese still felt for their former ruler.

The circumstances under which, in Act II, scene 1 of the play, Antonio sets about persuading Sebastian to kill his brother Alonso, are, it is true, very different. It is, however, worth noting a couple of similarities. Just as Antonio used Prospero as a ladder in his rise to power and discarded him when he could be of no further use, so now — having accomplished with his aid all that could be accomplished — he is about to cast Alonso aside and take up with a more profitable ally. Indeed, he does not even have to raise with Sebastian the price of his confederacy; just as they are about to dispatch the sleeping figures of Alonso and Gonzalo, Sebastian makes the offer that Antonio has been waiting to hear:

> Draw thy sword. One stroke
> Shall free thee from the tribute which thou payest
>
> (II.1.297–298)

We should notice, too, the way in which Antonio, almost instinctively, uses the opportunities that present themselves to him. He realises immediately the possibilities of the situation in which the King and his other companions are overcome with drowsiness, while he and Sebastian remain fully awake. With Ferdinand undoubtedly drowned and Claribel satisfactorily occupied with the cares of state in Tunis ('ten leagues beyond man's life'), Sebastian would naturally succeed to the throne of Naples if anything were to happen to Alonso. And Alonso is as deeply asleep in body, before their very eyes, as Prospero was morally asleep all those years ago in Milan.

There is little to choose between these two villains in terms of nastiness. From the very start of the play, Shakespeare has

been at pains to establish the unpleasantness of their characters. In the opening storm, while the King and Ferdinand
respond to the request of the Boatswain that they 'keep below',
Antonio and Sebastian insist on returning to the deck of the
ship, hindering the work of the mariners and berating them for
drunkenness. They are, of course, accompanied at this time by
Gonzalo, but it is worth pointing out that the tone and manner
that he adopts in speaking to the Boatswain and his men are
very different from those employed by Antonio and Sebastian.
Later in the play, during Act II, while Gonzalo and Adrian are
attempting to divert Alonso from his grief over the supposed loss
of Ferdinand, they are entirely cynical, commenting that the
King 'receives comfort like cold porridge'. Their cynicism turns
to outright mockery when Gonzalo begins to recount what he
would do if he were king of the island. They have no conscience
about their attempt on the King's life, and have an excuse ready
when they are caught, with drawn swords, by the waking
Alonso:

> Whiles we stood here securing your repose,
> Even now, we heard a hollow burst of bellowing
> Like bulls, or rather lions. Did't not wake you?
> It struck mine ear most terribly.

> (II.1.314–317)

And, having failed in this first attempt, they look for further
opportunities to encompass their design later in the play. When,
in Act III, scene 3, their companions are once again dropping
with exhaustion, Antonio urges Sebastian not, on account of one
setback, to 'forego the purpose/ That you resolved t'effect'. And
Sebastian replies:

> The next advantage
> Will we take throughly.

> (III.3.14–15)

Nor are the two villains abashed by Prospero's revelation, in the
final scene of the play, that he knows all about their conspiracy:

> But you, my brace of lords, were I so minded,
> I here could pluck his highness' frown upon you,
> And justify you traitors. At this time

I will tell no tales.

SEBASTIAN (*aside*)   The devil speaks in him.

(V.1.126–129)

When, furthermore, Prospero offers his brother forgiveness for his past crimes, Antonio remains malevolently silent.

If, in the eyes of a Jacobean audience, the idea of manipulating society and the way it is organised by means of an act of usurpation was entirely unacceptable, the same could not be said for the notion of doing so by means of a contract of marriage. Particularly among the upper classes, marriage meant not just the union of a loving couple, but also the transfer of titles, lands and fortunes from one family to another. At the end of *The Tempest*, as well as being restored to his own dukedom, Prospero has the gratification of knowing that, as Ferdinand's wife, Miranda will one day be Queen of Naples, and that her heirs will be rulers of the city in their own right. Gonzalo sums up the position memorably:

> Was Milan thrust from Milan that his issue
> Should become kings of Naples? O, rejoice
> Beyond a common joy, and set it down
> With gold on lasting pillars. In one voyage
> Did Claribel her husband find at Tunis,
> And Ferdinand her brother found a wife
> Where he himself was lost; Prospero his dukedom
> In a poor isle, and all of us ourselves
> When no man was his own.

(V.1.205–213)

In returning to Milan as its righful ruler, Prospero is of course aware that he must foreswear those studies that caused him to lose control of the city in the first place. In the Epilogue to the play, he tells the audience that his magic arts have now been cast aside, that such strength as he possesses is entirely his own. His island 'household' is in the process of being disbanded: he will soon be leaving Miranda with her new husband in Naples; he gives Ariel one final commission, after which his tricksy spirit will be 'to the elements/ . . . free'. Only Caliban's future remains in doubt. He accepts Prospero's offer of pardon for his misdeeds in return for carrying out further domestic chores in his master's cell, promising to 'be wise here-after/ And seek for grace'. There is, however, no suggestion that his island will be returned to him on Prospero's departure. Similarly, although Alonso has survived their attempt on his life and crown, there is no indication that Antonio and Sebastian acknowledge or regret the error of their ways. It does not require too great an exercise of the imagination to see them causing further trouble for him in the future.

In the course of *The Tempest*, then, we see a widespread upsetting of social order and organisation. Though the status quo is in part restored at the play's conclusion, there are some things that, it is clear, will never be quite the same again.

AFTERTHOUGHTS

1

Could *you* describe Prospero's island?

2

What do you understand by the term 'social organisation'?

3

What differing attitudes to usurpation are described in this essay? In what ways is the concept central to Adams's argument?

4

Adams concludes that, after the events of *The Tempest*, the status quo will 'never be quite the same again'. Does he see this as a good thing or a bad?

Stephen Siddall

*Stephen Siddall is Head of English at
the Leys School, Cambridge.*

ESSAY

The Tempest:
confinement and release

As you from crimes would pardoned be
Let your indulgence set me free.

(Epilogue, lines 19–20)

With these words Prospero ends his appeal to the audience. The speech as a whole has been knotted and troubled, unlike the graceful tribute audiences had come to expect in other plays of the period from actors who had been their servants for two and a half hours and who had brought their story to a resolved conclusion. Here, though, the magician, who has exercised such unusual powers over people, finds himself alone in still being trapped by the stage and his role on it. The other characters (still oddly assorted in their differences of innocence, vice and matured goodness) have left for Naples — or, to put it another way, since the theatrical fiction is over, as actors they have returned to the tiring house to escape from the 'shadow' of their roles in *The Tempest*. Prospero, alone, hovers in the strangely blurred area between the play and real life, still in his Prospero's costume, still the troubled isolate who had planned to avoid the celebrations and retire to Milan to think about his death. He speaks here of confinement, despair, inadequate powers, and seems to hope for release in extinction. But he also asks for 'the help of your good hands' — i.e. the generous response from onlookers in real life to relieve someone in distress. In the context of a play, this mention of hands is to the applause which marks the dividing line between finished illusion and the return to reality; it also acknowledges and justifies the work of an actor, whose life is spent vulnerably in the world of theatrical shadows. Also evident in these final lines is the shift from hands-in-applause to hands-in-prayer. Prospero (as 'God' in the play) offered forgiveness to his court victims; now, as supplicant, he begs it from his audience; and they, in turn, in their life outside the play, need Christian forgiveness. Like all human beings, they/we are confined by our mortality, which is the world of sin and virtue, inescapably mingled, into which we are born. The spirit is trapped for a lifetime's span within the body and made restless by its carnal imprisonment. It longs for the pure and uncomplicated heaven which was its origin and proper milieu.

Though *The Tempest* is not overtly Christian, it makes use of such Christian assumptions in a Christian culture. One of these is that being human is to be poised halfway between the extremes of pure spirit and base animal. The comedy of *A Midsummer Night's Dream* uses this tripartite view in the division into (a) fairies, (b) courtiers and lovers, (c) workmen, and indicates that each level has the potential through visions and humiliations to make bewildering contact with a higher or lower stratum. Hence the passionate extremes of joy, hatred, despair and wonder in that volatile play. *The Tempest* presents a far more elusive spirit world centring on Ariel; then a far more varied human world with more overt moral possibilities in the disorientated court party; then the single 'person' of Caliban at the brute level. Shakespeare identifies his higher and lower with the four elements: Ariel is air and fire, while Caliban comes from the slime of earth and water. As with *A Midsummer Night's Dream*, the world of the play is separated from the normal conditions of real life (in this case by a storm rather than an enchanted forest), and the action takes place in a fantastical environment. Characters in the middle, or human, level are faced with a paradox: they are free from the restrictive conventions of their real-life hierarchies and customs, yet this loosening brings aimless wandering, distress and terror. At the upper and lower levels, too, there is both confinement and release. Ariel spent twelve years imprisoned in a cloven pine until released by Prospero, whilst Caliban's fortunes are reversed — he was lord of the isle and sustained by the black arts of Sycorax until enslaved by Prospero. But these roles they play in their master's service — free spirit and shackled slave — are subject to some contradiction. Ariel feels restless even within his new freedom, whilst Caliban has visions and a sensitive ear for the island's music that allow him to escape in his imagination beyond the conditions of his slavery.

From Ariel's first appearance there are curious incongruities about his freedom and servitude, as there are about Prospero in his relationship to this servant. Ariel's first words (I.2.189), 'All hail, great master', acknowledge subjection, followed by enormous relish in the energy of what he has just achieved:

> Now on the beak,
> Now in the waist, the deck, in every cabin
> I flamed amazement.
>
> (I.2.196–198)

The wild terror he stirred in his victims he then contrasts with the stillness that followed. Immediately, without clear warning, he makes his protests about the tasks he has seemed to enjoy:

> Is there more toil? Since thou dost give me pains,
> Let me remember thee what thou hast promised,
> Which is not yet performed me.
>
> (I.2.242–244)

Prospero's angry reply is but one example of the troubled relationships he seems to undergo with everyone in the play. Perhaps his need for Ariel is greater than for others, even Miranda, not merely because Ariel has such extraordinary powers of performance and manipulation, but because the possibility of contact with this spirit seems to be both offered and impossible. The actual relationship between them is based on frustration on both sides. In this first scene, Prospero's frustration drives him into long stories of others' misdeeds: in the first — to Miranda — he speaks of himself as victim of political corruption, whilst in this — to Ariel — he was the avenger. By his art he released Ariel from the aggressive magic of Sycorax.

By rights, therefore, Ariel should be grateful and serve uncomplainingly. But he appears puzzled by the expectation of such response; he is not human and therefore human gratitude is outside his nature. The nearest he comes to this or any real warmth is in the moment of describing Gonzalo's distress in Act V:

> His tears runs down his beard like winter's drops
> From eaves of reeds. Your charm so strongly works 'em
> That if you now beheld them your affections
> Would become tender.

(V.1.16–19)

Perhaps in these lines he is recognising tenderness, feeling for others, as a high ideal; perhaps too he senses the difficulty Prospero has in achieving such responses, when he sees more commonly in his master's behaviour, trouble, indignation, anger and threat. Prospero learns something from Ariel at this point and determines to feel forgiving to those who have wronged him. However, Ariel is 'but air', and in showing 'a touch, a feeling/ Of their afflictions' he is not experiencing warmth — he is simply an intelligent, observant onlooker who knows what is proper for humans to feel, just as he knows that, as a spirit, he is an isolate and that his instinct is for freedom, even freedom from those feelings which enlarge and enrich human beings. The obvious example of human love in action is the way Ferdinand and Miranda are absorbed in each other; at their encounters both Prospero and Ariel are onlookers, set apart from the experience. In Act IV Prospero is about to bestow some vanity of his art in the masque of fertility which will celebrate Miranda's worth and Ferdinand's devotion tested. Ariel, about to stage-manage the masque, pauses for moment, observes the human lovers and questions Prospero about his feelings, 'Do you love me, master? No?' The two questions in this line (IV.1.48) may suggest that Prospero is aware of his isolation but unable quite to express the strange dependence that a master may have for his servant when that servant is both delicate and detached. There is no sense here that Ariel feels love for Prospero — it is more a benevolent curiosity. Neither does the question nor its answer absorb Ariel's interest for long. His nature, like the imagery that describes him, is protean — all is movement, merging, constant transformation, and an absence of definable self beyond the basic instinct for freedom, which his name implies, which he is continually promised in the second half of the play, and which he achieves as Prospero speaks his final words to the court party.

Ariel's disappearance leaves Prospero empty:

> Now my charms are all o'erthrown,
> And what strength I have's mine own.

(Epilogue, lines 1–2)

Caliban, by contrast, remains an awkward presence. Prospero would like to be free of him, perhaps as any aspiring and sensitive human being would wish to lose the pressing claims of his baser nature. Since this play is partly about the protagonist's creative powers, there is a sense that Ariel and Caliban are not only independent characters, but also represent opposing aspects of an individual personality, so that *The Tempest* is also an account of Prospero as Everyman. He admits his inescapable link with Caliban: 'This thing of darkness/ I acknowledge mine' (V.1.75). Caliban remains intractable as he was at the start and so is part of the failure that Prospero feels in the last speech. Like Ariel, Caliban responds only to his instincts, but in his case these are earth-bound. He showed Prospero the physical qualities of the island, but was unable to respond to grace, reason or civilised values. Instead he approached Miranda as an animal and was thereafter punished by the discipline proper to animals. Although he regards Prospero as a scheming coloniser who has deprived him of his rightful inheritance, this experience does not educate him; he remains equally gullible when he meets the next 'deliverer'. Prospero had been armed with magic arts: now Stephano is equipped with alcohol and is therefore worshipped too until the end of the play brings Caliban to the end of another delusion. Stephano's wine gives its slaves the illusion of power, imagination and purpose as they all three establish their little kingdom (a parody of Gonzalo's fantasy) and aim to supplant Prospero. Caliban's slavish nature requires that he have someone to worship, but his adoration — far from making Stephano a magnanimous king — simply feeds his arrogance and materialistic desires. And so, although the butler feels his imagination soaring, his real progress in the play is a downward slope from rational humanity. Eventually, the three fools are driven through mud and briars; distracted by superficial finery, they jabber like animals and are finally deposited at the feet of the court party. There they demonstrate the potential to baseness inherent in human nature, to the disgust of the right-thinking onlookers and to the mockery of the two cynics, Antonio and Sebastian.

These two also thwart the harmony and reconciliation which should conclude the play. They are like the Caliban group in remaining unsusceptible to generous impulses, though very different in their courtly elegance. The stage picture at this point will contrast their panache with the squalid clumsiness they are mocking. Like Stephano and Caliban, they have granted themselves an illusion of power and purpose in their conspiracy to supplant and murder a rightful ruler, but in being more devious they present a far greater threat. If Caliban represents the open brutishness of nature, Antonio and Sebastian (when they eventually cope with the strangeness of their new surroundings) establish a more political partnership that belongs to the 'civilised' world they have left. In this respect, Shakespeare is using the traditions of pastoral literature that describe a contrast between stylish courtly corruption and the sort of natural simplicity that, in this play, is seen in Miranda. As Antonio and Sebastian draw closer together, the others in the court party remain separate in their wanderings. Alonso is alone in his grief, Ferdinand is drawn by music to his own discovery, Gonzalo is generously concerned but makes little contact with his king. They all submit to their separate circumstances, whilst the two villains create a style of speech that at times appears almost like a private code. Their sly circumlocutions also feed their self-importance; they convince themselves that, far from being trapped in an unfamiliar world, they can control their own destinies. In this they are just as deluded as the Caliban group, but more worrying because their status and breeding should open their minds to the 'clearer understanding' that reaches the others. Instead they stand apart and sneer at whatever seems vulnerable — at Gonzalo in the first scene, at Caliban, Stephano and Trinculo in the last.

Alonso is the only character to be altered by the play's

strange experiences. His former wickedness is punished through the tempest in his losing Ferdinand. He is then confined by deep grief, so that he fails to respond either to the attempt on his life or to Gonzalo's encouraging support. His apparently aimless journey through the isle is in fact a spiritual journey that leads him through terrifying experiences like the harpies' banquet and Ariel's accusation, to Prospero's cave and eventual release. He stands 'spell-stopped', and as Prospero surveys their moral state, the imagery speaks of light melting the darkness, of 'ignorant fumes' giving way to 'clearer reason' and of a 'muddy shore' which will be cleansed and filled with 'the approaching tide'. These images imply a very limited and confined moral existence up to this point, and an enlarging freedom which will be granted when they wake from their trance. Alonso then asks for forgiveness; he is rewarded by seeing his son and Miranda, whose union promises a rich future. In returning to Naples, Alonso's sense of wonder will continue as he hears Prospero's story, and he will take with him the benefits of imaginative release granted by his island experience. He has thus been educated not by direct instruction or by anything that directly reached his conscious state, but via his imagination while in a state of trance.

Ariel introduces Ferdinand also in a trance:

> . . . cooling of the air with sighs
> In an odd angle of the isle, and sitting,
> His arms in this sad knot.

(I.2.222–224)

The picture demonstrates a man locked in grief and despair. He is then given a strange substitute life by the music he hears. It leads him to Miranda, soothes him 'with its sweet air' and speaks of the value (in coral and pearl) that the 'sea-change' will have given both father and son. His grief dissolves in wonder, and then the more so when he sees Miranda. Each is held by the beauty of the sight, but the moment is immediately dashed when Prospero reacts harshly. Ferdinand first finds himself physically restricted — his 'nerves are in their infancy again' — and then subdued to the tests imposed. As a prince he has come to expect privilege and dignity, but to achieve Miranda he must submit voluntarily to acting the role of another Caliban and carrying logs like a slave. It is Miranda who expresses indignation at such servitude: Ferdinand comes to accept the new values which the new experiences are giving him. He declares that his losses:

> . . . are but light to me,
> Might I but through my prison once a day
> Behold this maid. All corners else o'th'earth
> Let liberty make use of. Space enough
> Have I in such a prison.

(I.2.490–494)

As the hero of a myth, suddenly switching from prince to slave, he humbles himself, like Sir Gareth, the Arthurian knight who suffered indignities to prove his worth. The temporary breakdown of rank is symbolic and is designed to strengthen its resumption and the value of his marriage. Shakespeare creates a similar role for Florizel, the young hero-prince in *The Winter's Tale*; he too reacts with instinctive pride when threatened, and (in play) dresses as a humble shepherd in the presence of his princess. At the end of both plays both royal couples have been tested and justified — Florizel and Perdita at the ceremony of Hermione's restoration, Ferdinand and Miranda as performers in their own ceremony of the chess game. The paradox of Ferdinand's progress is that he must undergo a physical slavery in order to be pronounced free of the moral dangers inherent in his courtly origin. The true freedom in his marriage to Miranda is made possible only when the Court, now purged of vice (in the person of the prince) meets Nature, in the grace and simplicity of Miranda. The staged masque shows that they will be granted:

> Honour, riches, marriage blessing
> Long continuance and increasing

(IV.1.106–107)

Venus and Cupid have been dismissed, since the combination of moral discipline and natural grace have triumphed over blindness, lust and anarchy. These vices have promised an illusory freedom to some characters in the play, but the celebration for Ferdinand and Miranda shows that true freedom is to be found elsewhere.

The masque of the three goddesses is one of three formally staged ceremonies in *The Tempest* — the banquet and game of chess precede and follow it. All three may be seen as moments of theatrical restraint within a play in which the meanings are elusive and suggestive and whose limits are marked by the storm at the start and by Prospero's troubled shedding of theatrical fiction at the end. In between he has been the great theatrical manager, the creator of visions. These three moments are the most formal and they share an important paradox: it is the very constraint of the staging that permits the imaginative release that the whole play has been encouraging. In the 'banquet' the restraint is even tighter, as the lords are all physically trapped, before then receiving the message that seems to come from outside their own time and space. There is strange music, they are told of a guilty past and desolate future, and threatened by the vast imagery of 'the powers' in league with the sea that has belched them on to the island. This ceremony concludes the first, and more severe, half of the play, with its focus on guilt and punishment.

The second half stresses hope and reconciliation, and the two ceremonies here include Ferdinand and Miranda. The masque of goddesses is performed for the lovers as audience; we watch them watching and with them we gather the formally presented meanings, before Prospero roughly breaks the theatrical spell. In the last ceremony it is the lords who are brought to the edge of the mystery; they are the onstage audience, while the lovers have moved into a new plane of illusion and have become participants in the play within the play. Chess is a most formal, disciplined and aristocratic encounter, and as they engage in it they submit to its rules, and yet are playful too. There is wonder on both sides of the divide between fiction and audience. Alonso is astonished to see his son and the 'goddess' who is with him; Miranda, as she steps out of the 'frame', wonders at the 'brave new world' that she sees. Each in fact is both audience and performance for the other. All three staged moments, therefore, operate according to the rules of art and play tantalisingly with the edges of illusory worlds; also, all three offer strange experiences to their audiences whose wonder frees the imagination towards moral growth.

Prospero has set up the conditions for enlightenment and

release in all the characters he has controlled. But this control has always been limited: he has had the power to punish and discipline his opponents, he has been able to bring Ferdinand face to face with Miranda and the court party to his cell. Beyond this he can do little. People continue to exist in their moral varieties — they can't be compelled to love, repent or forgive. Generous impulses cannot be planted from outside on natures that will not receive them. To this extent Prospero has failed. His one great success is the union of Ferdinand and Miranda, but even his role as partially controlling onlooker is touched with sadness, because their togetherness highlights his isolation. This was evident from the first scene in which each of his four encounters (with Miranda, Ariel, Caliban and Ferdinand) contained elements of irritation and harshness. Prospero seems destined to live outside human relationships, but, unlike Ariel's, his nature can't easily accommodate isolation. And at the end, when hearing of the lords' distress, he is urged into a forgiving spirit, he seems to find the *concept* of reconciliation easier to accept than its *feeling*. His 'nobler reason' struggles with only partial success against his 'fury' so that his words to Antonio are strained and grudging:

> For you, most wicked sir, whom to call brother
> Would even infect my mouth, I do forgive
> Thy rankest fault

(V.1.130–132)

In spite of his great powers and ideals as a Renaissance scholar, Prospero seems trapped by constrictions within his own nature. He has lived on a boundary between the world of men and spirits. From this eminence he has been able to judge, release and enlarge others, but for himself he has had to accept disappointment, in that he can never live in the world of the spirit and as a man he is fallible and subject to his passions. Eventually, he must turn to *his* masters, the audience, and asks to:

> . . . be relieved by prayer,
> Which pierces so, that it assaults
> Mercy itself, and frees all faults.

(Epilogue, lines 16–18)

AFTERTHOUGHTS

1

How useful do you find the comparison with *A Midsummer Night's Dream* in the second paragraph of this essay?

2

Siddall suggests that the play is 'an account of Prospero as Everyman' (page 83). What do you understand by this?

3

Compare Siddall's account of 'the three formally staged ceremonies in *The Tempest*' (page 87) with the analysis presented in Charles Moseley's essay.

4

Would you agree that this essay is based on character study? What arguments are there for and against character study being an appropriate way of approaching a dramatic text?

Nigel Smith
*Nigel Smith is Lecturer in English at
Keble College, Oxford.*

ESSAY

The Italian job: magic and Machiavelli in *The Tempest*

Shakespeare's Italy is always a dangerous place. Prospero, the
once and rightful Duke of Milan, has been supplanted by his
brother, who, as deputy for the bookish, retiring Prospero, is led
by his own ambition to believe that he is actually the Duke: 'To
have no screen between this part he played/ And him he played
it for, he needs will be/ Absolute Milan' (I.2.107–109). Though
The Tempest takes place on Prospero's enchanted island, the
purpose of the action is to put Prospero back as Duke of Milan.
The play is concerned with Italy, and with the rivalries and
factions both within and between Renaissance Italian courts and
states. While *The Tempest* clearly has other features — such as
concerns with colonialism and the discovery of other peoples in
the New World, and with magic — the drama returns to Italy.
In some senses we never leave Italy. In the discussion which
follows, I shall show why Shakespeare uses Italy in *The
Tempest*, and what this aspect contributes to the play at large.

   The great Italian historian and political theorist Francesco
Guicciardini (1483–1540) produced his *Storia d'Italia* in retire-
ment at the end of his career between 1537 and 1540. This
monumental work tells of the ravages which befell the Italian
states after 1490, through the ambitions of powerful aristocratic

families and the interference of foreign powers. Guicciardini is a cool analyst and a sharp observer of men in power. He had in fact been an adviser to the Medici families and had helped to have Cosimo I elected Duke of Florence. Against Guicciardini's advice, Cosimo had yielded Pisa, Livorno and Florence to the Holy Roman Emperor in 1537, and it was then that the historian retired to write what he claimed was an objective history of the motivations of the men who held destiny in their hands.

Guicciardini tells us that in 1490 Italy was in a period of peace and prosperity. Under the auspices of Lorenzo de Medici, Florence, Milan and Naples were in an alliance against Venice which maintained the balance of power and hence equilibrium. But this peace was shattered within three years by French claims to the throne of Naples and a French invasion of Italy with the aim of securing that claim. Uncannily, some of the major figures in this history have names very similar to those of the characters in *The Tempest*. The King of Naples was called Ferdinand, just like the son of the King of Naples in Shakespeare's play: a son who was of course intended one day to be his father's successor. The son in Guicciardini was called Alphonso, famous for his military prowess, while in Shakespeare, it is the father, the King of Naples who is called Alonso. Shakespeare could well have seen and read the *Storia d'Italia*, as it was translated into English and published in 1579, 1599 and 1618. Another Italian history tells of a Milanese lieutenant, Prospero Adorno, who became Duke of Genoa, fell into an alliance with Naples, and was eventually overthrown and expelled.[1]

However, Shakespeare was attracted not only by names. The Italian life of cities and courts had fascinated English people for over a century by the time *The Tempest* was first performed in 1611. The Italians were considered more sophisticated in every respect than the provincial and insolent English. English poets imitated Italian lyricists and epic writers

---

[1] See William Thomas, *The Historie of Italie* (1549), fol. 181ᵛ, and William Shakespeare, *The Tempest*, edited by Stephen Orgel (Oxford, 1987), 'Introduction', pp.42–43.

in order to dignify their own language, while English commentators looked aghast at the sophistication, and sometimes uncomfortable realism, of Italian political commentary. At the same time, the political and sexual corruption of the Italian courts fascinated playwrights and audiences alike in England. John Webster's plays, *The White Devil* (1612) and *The Duchess of Malfi* (1614), are among the best examples of this fashion, as well as Shakespeare's own earlier masterpiece *Othello*. But this interest in the rage and violence of Italian passion had gone on for at least ten years by the time Shakespeare came to write *The Tempest* in 1610–1611. I believe that for one of his last plays (his third or fourth to last), he turned to Italian history and historical writing to find new insights for his drama, to take what the Italians themselves had learnt from the mayhem of the late fifteenth and early sixteenth centuries.

The Italian political thinkers searched in their writing for the conditions of stable government, against the reality of foreign invasion and the gradual replacement in Italy of republics by seigneurial rule. Republican 'liberty' was seen as worthy of defence against the possibility of corrupt rule by one man. A good governor, be he prince or magistrate, should have sufficient virtuous qualities to overcome the stumbling blocks which fortune left in his path. This was in fact the message of the most famous of the Italian Renaissance minds, Niccolò Machiavelli (1469–1527), but whereas his contemporaries (including Guicciardini) thought of virtue as a wholly positive quality, Machiavelli tore away the veils of illusion and ventured to suggest that true *virtù* involved not only courage, but also stealth and dissimulation.[2] For the sake of political stability, it might be necessary sometimes to murder one's opponents, a suggestion which produced in England the frightening image of the stage Machiavel, one quite at odds with Machiavelli's own intentions.

Prospero's 'art' is just such a Machiavellian achievement, even though it is cast in the form of a magical act. The first time

---

[2] For the best general account of Italian Renaissance political thought, see Quentin Skinner, *The Foundations of Modern Political Thought*, 2 vols (Cambridge, 1978), pp. 69–189, and especially pp. 128–138, 180–186 on Machiavelli.

we become aware of this is when we see Prospero making the best of Fortune, when it has brought the ship close to the island: 'By accident most strange, bountiful Fortune,/ Now my dear lady, hath mine enemies/ Brought to this shore' (I.2.178–180). Prospero might appear to be addressing Miranda, but he is addressing the classical goddess Fortuna, over which *virtù* should have power. But his statements here mirror precisely the ambivalence which the Italians felt about fortune. Prospero goes on to say that in order to make the most of fortune, he must 'depend upon/ A most auspicious star' (I.2.181–182). This refers to Prospero's special knowledge of nature (here astrology), so that he is both impelled to use his skills to exploit fortune, and so overcome his previous bad fortune, while at the same time suggesting that he has no final power over fortune or fate. Just so did the Italian political thinkers, Guicciardini and even more so Machiavelli, doubt the unlimited powers of *virtù*.

But if man's capacity to escape the blows of fortune is questioned, Prospero is careful and eager to seize his chance. His performance is a supreme act of statesmanship right down to the secretive withholding of information from Miranda until the proper moment: 'The hour's now come' (I.2.36). Prospero's anger at his loss is imparted during his explanation of how he came to be deposed by his brother. Like the Duke in *Measure for Measure*, he devoted too much time to private study, and let Antonio his brother be deputy. Antonio quickly learnt the art of courtly politics ('who t'advance, and who/ To trash for overtopping, new created/ The creatures that were mine' — I.2.80–82) until he had formidable influence and popularity. With the help of the King of Naples, Antonio, believing that he was the rightful Duke Milan, had Prospero and Miranda carried out of the city. They were not murdered, for that would have been unpopular with the Milanese, but were cast adrift in a rotten boat. Prospero becomes increasingly ill-tempered during his recounting of this history, even thinking that Miranda is not listening. Such discomfort seems to stem from the fact that there has been betrayal by a brother and that one man, Antonio, should have wished to be 'absolute' ruler. Before the coup, Prospero is but one among many, the 'prime duke', but not the only one. Milan would seem to be in the hands of an aristocracy, albeit of one family. But this shared rule is ended by the deputy

Antonio's ambition. For Machiavelli, the process of history was a cycle in which princely rule by one was replaced by aristocratic faction, only to be replaced by a popular democracy, which would in time revert back to princely rule.[3] The cycle in *The Tempest* is moving in the opposite direction, but it is one much more consistent with the trend in the Italian city-states, as republics were replaced by princely despotisms.

The title and first two scenes of the play reflect these concerns through a symbolism common in European habits of political thinking. The ship in the storm in I.1 is the familiar medieval image of the ship of state tossed in the stormy sea of fortune, fate or Providence. The storm itself seems to suggest Fortuna, and this would have been associated in the Italian mind with the apocalyptic imagery which accompanied accounts of the rise or fall of republics. The very word 'tempest', echoing the Latin *tempus* (time) bears also the dual sense of 'temperance' and 'temper', the two sides of Prospero's character which are revealed to us as he seeks to control, to educate and to regain his lost state.

Machiavelli thought that the best state would be one in which there was a mixture of monarchy, aristocracy and democracy. This would be the ideal 'republic'. At the opposite end entirely, *The Tempest* reveals the further taint of seigneurial ambition. Shipwrecked and washed up on the shore, Antonio tries to persuade Sebastian to kill his brother, Alonso the King of Naples. Sebastian would then be king, which would suit Antonio since he is in debt to Alonso for services rendered in Antonio's own rise to power. Helped by Antonio, Sebastian would be in Milan's debt, thereby reversing the situation at the start of the play. Antonio tempts Sebastian in the same terms used by Prospero to explain his strategy. Sebastian is letting his fortune 'sleep', and his ambition will not see that with Ferdinand supposedly drowned and his niece, Claribel, safely married off in Tunis, Sebastian is but a deadly sword's stroke from the crown.

Fortunately, the 'open-eyed conspiracy' is circumvented by Ariel's whispered warnings. The courtiers are reserved for a

---

[3] Machiavelli, *Discorsi*, 1.2.

further visitation by Ariel in the guise of a harpy who tells Antonio, Alonso and Sebastian that they will be punished for deposing Prospero. The audience knows that this is all part of Prospero's design to regain his throne and that Ariel is an extension of his will. The characters accept that the harpy is an agent of Destiny. The scene is Machiavellian on two accounts. First, Prospero is using a system of belief in the supernatural in order to control those in his power, just as Machiavelli saw that religion was a form of social control. Secondly, the courtiers respond in two differing ways which correspond to Machiavellian analysis. Alonso, full of grief for his son's supposed death, accepts the harpy's message, and in order to avoid 'lingering perdition' trapped on the 'desolate isle' goes off to kill himself. Antonio and Sebastian, however, display their *virtù* and prepare to join battle with the fiends they see before them.

Bewildered and confused, Prospero appears before the courtiers in his former costume as Duke of Milan. Having reassumed his former throne, and having arranged the fortunate marriage between his daughter and Alonso's son, Ferdinand, he is able to forgive (but only just) his brother, as well as to welcome Alonso and the kind Gonzalo. This final act of statecraft is represented by the revelation of Ferdinand and Miranda playing chess, the apt and current image for the complications of international relations and the use of marriage alliances within them.[4] It was the claim to thrones through marriages which partly tore apart Renaissance Italy, but Prospero has the clever means to fashion the perfect match of nobility and virtue.

So Prospero's aims are brilliantly fulfilled. But in achieving them, he has undoubtedly relied upon the services of Ariel. The language which dominates the exchanges between Prospero and Ariel reveals the limits of freedom which are necessary for any political order to flourish. Here, the play contains an exploration of 'liberty' and 'freedom' as they were understood by the Italians. 'What is't thou canst demand?' asks Prospero. 'My liberty' is Ariel's reply (I.2.245). In thinking that Stephano and Trinculo will liberate him from the severe regime of Prospero, Caliban

---

4 See Bryan Loughrey and Neil Taylor, 'Ferdinand and Miranda at Chess', *Shakespeare Survey*, 35 (1982), pp.113–118.

exclaims: 'Ban, Ban, Cacaliban/ Has a new master — get a new man!/ Freedom, high-day! High-day, freedom! Freedom, high-day, freedom!' (II.2.180–182). In both cases, there is a paradox in the origins of their servitude to Prospero. Ariel had been imprisoned in a tree by Caliban's mother, Sycorax. He is in debt to Prospero for being freed, yet that freedom is also a condition of further servitude to Prospero until Prospero himself is freed from the island. Caliban is left on the island alone after the death of his mother. Prospero gives him language and a measure of cultivation, but this only enables Caliban to perceive that he is a slave, and to think that the island is his by inheritance from his mother.

Just so did the Italians, particularly Machiavelli, see political society not so much as a part of virtue founded upon loyalty and service as a series of tensions between individuals and classes in which constraints interacted with necessities to produce energetic achievement.[5] There is energy in the frustration, resentment and aggravation which exists between Prospero, Ariel and Caliban. Prospero is greatly aggrieved to think that Ariel has forgotten who freed him: 'Thou liest, malignant thing!' (I.2.257). Ariel is loyal but anxious to earn his freedom through his good service: Prospero is a kind of patron for the spirit. Caliban, who has attempted to rape Miranda, is but a 'poisonous slave', who must be controlled by magically inflicted tortures. Even Ferdinand must demonstrate his loyalty in slave-like service to Prospero before he is allowed to marry Miranda.

Most commentators have seen the Prospero-Caliban relationship as a reflection of European man's first encounters with the American Indian.[6] The learning of a language serves only the ends of Prospero the coloniser. Caliban can only serve and swear. Deprived of his rights and his property (though he only knows about this through Prospero's education) he is truly exploited. The cynical attempt by Stephano and Trinculo to

---

[5] Machiavelli, *Discorsi*, 1.4.
[6] For a recent account, see Paul Brown, '"This thing of darkness I acknowledge mine": *The Tempest* and the discourse of colonialism', in Jonathan Dollimore and Alan Sinfield (eds), *Political Shakespeare. New Essays in Cultural Materialism* (Manchester, 1985), pp.48–71.

persuade Caliban to help them murder Prospero is only another example of the exploitative attitude. While this may be so, there is a dimension to this which is closer to home than the New World. Prospero operates power relationships with different degrees of restraint in them in order to further the marvellous achievement of his 'art'. Such relationships seem essential to the good rule of the prince, to the successful exercise of *virtù*. Against this reality is set the topsy-turvy utopian vision of Gonzalo, who, stranded and away from courtly corruption, sees an end to exploitation:

> I'th'commonwealth I would by contraries
> Execute all things. For no kind of traffic
> Would I admit; no name of magistrate.
> Letters should not be known. Riches, poverty,
> And use of service, none. Contract, succession,
> Bourn, bound of land, tilth, vineyard, none.
> No use of metal, corn, or wine, or oil.
> No occupation; all men idle, all,
> And women too, but innocent and pure.
> No sovereignty

(II.1.150–159)

The very use of the word 'contraries' points to the idea of opposition creating activity, but here we have a society flat and lifeless through the absence of vigorous laws and institutions. All things are held in common and crime does not exist, but there is no 'endeavour' because nature brings forth all food without effort. Over this world would Gonzalo rule, a world which is all nature and no culture. As Sebastian points out, there is a mammoth contradiction in having a king but no sovereignty. Human beings cannot forget what they are as social beings, and this involves the double bond of freedom in service. By using the language of sovereignty and contract in order to offer an alternative, Gonzalo has only affirmed the inevitability of such an order. He says he has raised the image of the never-never land to delight Sebastian and Antonio, but in fact he is playing the role of the sound humanist adviser, ironically pointing to an image of good governance by juxtaposing an image of how things are with how they never could be in order to inculcate a notion of how things might be in a better world. As matters stand,

Sebastian and Antonio are eagerly over-ambitious: 'You are gentlemen of brave mettle. You would lift the moon out of her sphere, if she would continue in it five weeks without changing' (II.1.185–187).

But Shakespeare has something to add to the set of political insights which he has borrowed. Throughout the play we become increasingly aware of the force of sleep and dream as a realm in which drab reality is seen through to a deeper level of truth. At first, we accept this as part of Prospero's magic, a convention in romance tradition by which changes of awareness are achieved. So, Miranda conveniently sleeps after learning of her origins, until Prospero needs her onstage again to meet Ferdinand. Alonso and Gonzalo sleep as an effect of the enchanted island, only to be woken by Ariel to warn them of the plot of Sebastian and Antonio. But by the end of the play, the dreams have become the very visions which human beings have of themselves and their creations, the realities which they build in their cities and courts. Prospero equates his magic with civilisation itself:

> The solemn temples, the great globe itself,
> Yea, all which it inherit, shall dissolve,
> And, like this insubstantial pageant faded,
> Leave not a rack behind. We are such stuff
> As dreams are made on; and our little life
> Is rounded with a sleep.   (IV.1.153–158)

Magic, political theory and statecraft are the same thing when set against mortality. Human beings create reality in the fictions by which they order themselves, and in these visions are fixed the necessities and limits of their freedom and servitude.

In this light, Prospero's ambivalent character begins to resemble that of a real fifteenth-century Duke of Milan, Philip, 'a prince of a subtill nature, wittie, a louer of travaile, couetouse to learne and to haue, and yet liberall in geuying, easie of pardonyng, but suspiciouse out of measure, and so light of credence, that many tymes he wrongefully ridde out of the waie the deerest friendes he hadd'.[7] In forgiving Sebastian, Prospero

---

[7] Thomas, op. cit., fol. 195^v.

represents a rejuvenated Philip who knows how to keep his friends. The 'liberty' (V.1.235) which the Boatswain discovers when the sailors are released by Prospero refers to the Italian word *libertà*, which meant both 'liberty' and 'liberality'.[8] Prospero displays a careful and politically astute generosity which will keep him in power as opposed to the 'liberality' of personal excess which Machiavelli said would lead rulers to exploit their subjects.[9] King Ferdinand of Naples was covetous, executing nobles who resisted his tax demands, while his son Alphonso, being equally unpopular, ran away with the royal treasury to Sicily.[10] Prospero's consummate magic represents what in Italian political writing would have been the highest achievement of *virtù*: to fight successfully a war without bloodshed.[11]

Throughout *The Tempest*, there are references to the great Latin epic by Virgil, the *Aeneid*, which tells of the journey of Aeneas from the burning city of Troy via an unsuccessful fling with Queen Dido in Carthage to found at last the city of Rome. Some critics have noticed that the courtiers are returning from the new Carthage, Tunis, after the marriage of Claribel, who becomes the renewed Dido. In this sense, Ferdinand becomes the new Aeneas, returning to Naples with a bride, which ensures the happy alliance of Milan and Naples, the two ends of Italy.[12] More than this, the play has given a renewed vision of Italian political theory, a positive appraisal of dissimulation in Prospero's art and his eventual mercy. Authority, liberty and freedom are explored and redefined. Republican or not, the court is purged, and blessed with a new marriage. Power, in service, or in freedom, is the exciting hope for the future after the bitter betrayals of the past.

---

[8] See William Thomas, *Principal Rules of the Italian Grammar, with a Dictionary* (1550), sig. Siv[v].

[9] Machiavelli, *Il Principe*, chapter 16.

[10] Thomas, *The Historie of Italie*, fols 134[v]–135[r].

[11] Yet another Prospero, surnamed Colonna, a Milanese captain, is the object of praise for his cunning skills which 'overcome more with industrie, with stratageme, and with temporising, then with the force or fortune of armes': Guicciardini, *The Historie of Guicciardini*, translated by Geoffrey Fenton (1599), p.703.

[12] See John Pitcher, 'A Theatre for the Future: *The Aeneid* and *The Tempest*', *Essays in Criticism*, 34 (1984), pp.193–215.

AFTERTHOUGHTS

1

What can a watcher or reader of *The Tempest* gain from a knowledge of Italian Renaissance political thought?

2

What do you understand by *virtù* (page 92)?

3

What significance does Smith attach to sleep and dream in *The Tempest* (page 98)?

4

Does this essay convince you that Shakespeare has 'borrowed' a 'set of political insights' (page 98)?

Robert Wilson

Robert Wilson teaches English at Merchant Taylors' School. He is the author of numerous school text books and editions, his most recent publication being Novels *(Longman, 1987)*

ESSAY

Prospero — the changer changed

Throughout *The Tempest* Prospero is the centre of the action, the initiator of the events which animate the play. He is the controller, the manipulator, the magician who has raised a tempest to bring the ship bearing the other principal characters to the island on which a transformation of human relationships and feelings takes place. He is the schemer who brings Miranda and Ferdinand together, observing their instant love for each other with satisfaction for he had planned just such a bonding. He has control over a powerful spirit, Ariel, who obeys all his commands and whose power produces the restorative trance that leads Ferdinand to Miranda in the early part of the play, frustrates the regicidal intentions of Sebastian and Antonio towards Alonso, King of Naples, confronts those three characters with their evil and produces a spectacular masque. Through Ariel, Prospero learns of and controls the evil plottings against himself of Caliban, Trinculo and Stephano. Also through Ariel, he draws all these characters into a circle in the final scene of the play. And within that circle, which is the symbol of wholeness and unity, a new order of living is effected: Prospero will be reinstated as Duke of Milan; Ferdinand and Miranda's marriage will result in the union of Milan and Naples; Alonso confesses his faults, and Antonio and Sebastian are warned to repress their evil machinations; Ariel is released, and Caliban is acknowledged for what he is. All this is managed and brought to fruition by Prospero, a magician of towering presence and power.

Yet this is but half the substance of the play, its external action, for Prospero is himself changed as the action unfolds, and partakes in the transformations of the final act. He is a part of the dramatic action, not standing outside it merely controlling the other characters, as a puppeteer might manoeuvre his puppets. Indeed the moments of greatest dramatic intensity are precisely those moments when our awareness of Prospero as manipulator coincides with our recognition of him as an unresolved, struggling human being with his own pilgrimage to pursue and his own inner transformation to effect through changes of feeling towards himself and others.

I shall first discuss how, in the early scenes, we come to recognise Prospero as fully involved and implicated in the dramatic tension of the play and how unresolved aspects of his life, arising from the experiences of earlier years, trouble him. I shall then turn to the play's final episodes and consider how Prospero is changed by two closely related realisations: firstly, that evil is active in the world and must be managed, not ignored; and secondly, that he must take his place alongside the rest of erring humanity and acknowledge the proper limits of that creaturely condition.

The duality in our awareness of Prospero is established within the first few scenes. On one level he is the magician securely in control of the storm he has created, able to boast that:

> I have with such provision in mine art
> So safely ordered, that there is no soul —
> No, not so much perdition as an hair
> Betid to any creature in the vessel
> Which thou heard'st cry, which thou saw'st sink.

> (I.2.28–32)

So he reassures Miranda that he is absolute master of the situation. Yet, throughout the dialogue that follows, in which he tells her of their history, he is very much on edge. His inner agitation emerges in a sequence of demands that she pay attention to his story, unnecessary demands we may feel, for Miranda is the very soul of obedience and attentiveness and who could doubt her overwhelming desire to know more of her own background? She has, as Prospero remarks, asked him to tell their history on many previous occasions.

There is far more behind these schoolmasterly demands for attention than a desire that Miranda should understand. Each admonition — after his initial 'Obey and be attentive' — follows a reference to his brother, Antonio:

> My brother and thy uncle, called Antonio —
> I pray thee, mark me, that a brother should
> Be so perfidious! . . .

(I.2.66–68)

> Thy false uncle —
> Dost thou attend me?

(I.2.77–78)

A very particular type of attention is necessary if Prospero is *himself* to come to terms with this evil. It is as if he is projecting out on to Miranda and demanding from her the very attention that he himself needs to give to the existence of treachery and malicious evil, not merely as an abstract presence in the world but as embodied in one of the closest of all relationships, that with his own brother. His mind repeatedly moves around the problem. He goes on to describe Antonio as:

> The ivy which had hid my princely trunk,
> And sucked my verdure out on't.

(I.2.86–87)

And follows that up yet again with 'Thou attend'st not'. What is it that remains such a problem for Prospero? What is it that he needs to look at so closely? The metaphor he chooses here offers us a clue. Ivy does indeed grow against great trees and use them as a means of support. It may also obscure the appearance of the tree *but* it is not parasitic; it does not suck out the sap, the vigour, the 'verdure' of the tree. Prospero's misapplication of the metaphor reflects his, as yet, irrational attitude towards Antonio and his fear that he will be overwhelmed by evil if he comes into close relationship with it. The man who seems so clearly in charge of the events of the play is not in full possession of his own feelings, is not indeed fully aware of the lack of harmony and clarity within himself.

With this little hindsight, we may now see how even in his more confident initial statements, there is an underlying agitation which emerges as an irritable urgency, a hurrying energy suggesting that much is to be achieved in a short time. Look again at the quotation I cited from the start of this scene (I.2.28–32). Prospero's urgency results in a fragmentation of syntax and a compression of statements. He fails to finish his first sentence, 'there is no soul — '. 'Hurt' might complete the statement but in his excitement he is already finding another way of expressing his care of the travellers. Notice, too, the way he finishes his sentence. He says that not even a hair has been lost to:

> ... any creature in the vessel
> Which thou heard'st cry, which thou saw'st sink. Sit down.

In his exhilaration, Prospero thinks at the double, merging two statements into one and still leaving room in the same line to tell Miranda to sit and attend!

Before we leave this quotation, there is a different and very significant detail to pick up. Prospero's reference to his care for even the hairs on the heads of the victims of his storm reminds us of at least three biblical moments. When Jesus sent out the disciples to preach, he assured them of the infinite care of God for them: 'even the hairs of your head are all numbered' (Matthew 10:30) and when, towards the end of St Luke's Gospel, he talks of the turbulent future, he similarly reassures them, 'But not a hair of your head will perish' (Luke 21:18). When St Paul is about to be wrecked on Malta, he asserts God's care of the mariners by saying, 'Not a hair is to perish from the head of any of you' (Acts 27:34). This is also remarkably close to Ariel's report of the effects of the shipwreck later in the scene: 'Not a hair perished' (I.2.217). What all this amounts to is the implication that Prospero's power is more than a man should have. He has assumed the providential role of God. Is it right that a man should so equip himself with esoteric and hermetic (magic) arts that he plays God in his world? Prospero himself, in the final moments of the play, will answer this question, but for the moment it remains at issue, part of the unresolved tension that surrounds him and gives dramatic depth to his presence.

It is helpful to think of Prospero as a man who undergoes two powerfully transforming life-crises. A major change had happened some twelve years before the action of the play begins, but we witness the second crisis, brought to a head in the three or four hours during which the shipwrecked travellers are on the island. These two crises are intimately bound up together, the second being a replaying and deepening of some of the elements of the first. Prospero recalls in Act I, scene 2 how he came to leave Milan, rightly condemning himself for an excessive devotion to private and esoteric studies: we learn that he prized his books 'above my dukedom'. Abandoning his responsibilities for the proper execution of his duties, he developed only that part of himself which concerned the mind. This too exclusive concentration on thinking meant that other aspects of life got out of control and the result was the usurpation of his birthright by an evil brother whose activities should have been within Prospero's awareness. When we consider the development of his personality, we must conclude that twelve years of isolation from society, in the company of a girl who embodies the finest and most compassionate of feelings, have prepared him to realise what comfortable study could not, namely that a man must take responsibility for the lives of those who depend upon him, that feelings are as important as thoughts, and that the presence of evil in the world can only be squarely faced when responsibility and feelings are active. To spend one's life in a library is to avoid all of these issues. In *The Tempest*, we see, in the person of Prospero, a man finally assuming full human responsibility and acting upon his own felt compassion without blinkering himself against the reality of destructive evil.

No wonder that in the important second scene, which establishes the basis for the entire dramatic action, Prospero expresses his sense of the significance of the impending crisis in the most intense of terms:

> . . . by my prescience
> I find my zenith doth depend upon

A most auspicious star, whose influence
If now I court not, but omit, my fortunes
Will ever after droop.

(I.2.180–184)

The preparation of twelve years is about to be tested — for though in theory he may have changed, the reality of his compassion and capacity for confronting evil have yet to be tested.

I have said that some of the most satisfactory dramatic moments in the play are those where our sense of Prospero as controller of the action coincides with a realisation that he too is caught up in its events and subject to struggle and change. I shall turn now to the last phases of the play and to some of those moments.

One of the most delightful pauses in *The Tempest* is the masque which Prospero produces to entertain Ferdinand and Miranda and to celebrate their impending marriage. In music and in dance and in language rich with the fecund associations of the natural world, the action halts and we contemplate a love that transcends mere sensuality and love-play, for Venus and Cupid are explicitly excluded from these nuptial celebrations. Yet, in the midst of the dance of nymphs and reapers — of natural deities and ordinary country folk — Prospero, we are told in the stage direction, '*starts suddenly and speaks; after which, to a strange, hollow, and confused noise, they heavily vanish*'. The mood changes utterly and we see the magician in the full relishing and flourishing of his art all at once recognising that more serious matters have to be attended to:

I had forgot that foul conspiracy
Of the beast Caliban, and his confederates
Against my life.

(IV.1.139–141)

Just such a forgetfulness of the evil of the world had led to his expulsion from Milan and the ascendancy of Antonio; but here the masque, the indulgence in his art, the book-learnt escape through magic from more disturbing matters, has been only temporary. Indeed, Prospero's sudden recognition of an evil creeping towards him is very intense, so much so that Miranda says:

> Never till this day
> Saw I him touched with anger so distempered.

> (V.1.144–145)

The reaction that Miranda identifies is not quite what we might have expected. The violence of his anger seems excessive, far more than the mere irritation of having to deal with three troublesome characters, two of whom are complete fools and all three of whom he can so easily manage. Again we sense that something far more fundamental is producing an intense repugnance and frustration in Prospero. Nor is it dissipated when he has uttered one of the most beautiful and well-turned speeches in the whole of Shakespeare, the speech that dismisses the world as no more than an 'insubstantial pageant' and concludes with this reductive summary of human experience:

> We are such stuff
> As dreams are made on; and our little life
> Is rounded with a sleep.

> (IV.1.156–158)

It is calming for a moment perhaps to say that life is too transitory for us to be greatly disturbed about anything and that everything is unreal. Perhaps such sentiments put a little space between us and the challenging event that impends. But as a final summing-up of human life it will not do, for it thrusts us firmly into a state of *un*consciousness, of dream-material, and the whole tendency of this play is towards an increase of consciousness, a facing-up to reality, and to the bad as well as the good.

Of course Prospero knows this and, putting his eloquent philosophising behind him, he turns his 'beating mind' to the business in hand:

> We must prepare to meet with Caliban.

> (IV.1.166)

No longer can he avoid through philosophic retreat the confrontation with evil. And what is this Caliban?:

> A devil, a born devil, on whose nature
> Nurture can never stick; on whom my pains,
> Humanely taken, are all lost, quite lost.
>
> (IV.1.188–190)

The repetitions of 'devil' and 'lost' suggest the difficulty that Prospero has in accepting that there exists an irreducible, bestial element that cannot be refined by the civilised arts. Everything he has encountered he has tried to bring within the control that he has gained through his studies, but Caliban embodies that part of human nature that remains and must remain purely animal, sensual and instinctive. In his despair, Prospero goes on to say that:

> . . . as with age his body uglier grows,
> So his mind cankers.
>
> (IV.1.191–192)

It is a repulsive image but we know that, dangerous though he is, Caliban *is* susceptible to health-giving influences, not indeed those of human education, the 'nurture' of civilisation, but those of the natural world. He knows his island and all that it yields:

> I prithee, let me bring thee where crabs grow;
> And I with my long nails will dig thee pignuts
>
> (II.2.164–165)

and he responds sensitively to its beauties and its refreshing qualities:

> . . . the isle is full of noises,
> Sounds, and sweet airs, that give delight and hurt not.
>
> (III.2.136–137)

Prospero's verdict on Caliban is clearly not an objective nor true description of the creature; rather, it exposes his own problem, a problem that is not to be resolved until, in the final scene, he says:

> This thing of darkness I
> Acknowledge mine.
>
> (V.1.275–276)

In accepting that an intractable element of shadow, 'darkness' or malicious evil is a part of his being and must be lived with, Prospero becomes so much more of a man. Though he has successfully aspired to a transcendence and control of the material world, he must also recognise the animal in his own nature.

The fifth Act brings other, equally significant, changes in this changer, this manipulator of circumstances and people. It begins with Prospero back in full command of his feelings and plans:

> Now does my project gather to a head.
> My charms crack not, my spirits obey, and time
> Goes upright with his carriage.
>
> (V.1.1–3)

He boasts, he exults in the success of his plans, the application of his magic arts. Time can walk upright and make swift progress because so much has been accomplished and its burdens have been lessened. The evil men who plotted against Prospero in the past are all in his power: he has even abducted the son of one of the conspirators and betrothed him to his daughter. How will his vengeance proceed? Perhaps he will leave the unredeemed men on the island and, impounding their ship, sail off with his daughter and son-in-law. I raise the possibility simply to show how very undisclosed Prospero's plans are, even at this late stage of the action. It is as if he does not know how all his labours will end.

Clarification comes, appropriately, through Ariel, through the spirit of imagination and creativity:

> ARIEL   . . . if you now beheld them, your affections
>   Would become tender.
> PROSPERO   Dost thou think so, spirit?
> ARIEL   Mine would, sir, were I human.
> PROSPERO   And mine shall.
>
> (V.1.18–20)

Prospero's discovery comes through dialogue, not private meditation, through a vital sequence of brief potent statements, a confrontation with that imaginative faculty whose release had been his first act after arriving on the island. But here he is learning that the imagination is not simply a manipulative force, a way of fixing things, but rather the means whereby we understand each other. Imagination directed towards the lives of other people yields at first sympathy and, ultimately, understanding. So the spirit, over which Prospero has directed absolute control — in spite of Ariel's protestations against his servitude — here holds moral sway over Prospero.

The issue suddenly becomes very clear:

> Though with their high wrongs I am struck to th'quick,
> Yet with my nobler reason 'gainst my fury
> Do I take part.

(V.1.25–27)

Without diminishing their sins or his own outrage at the way he has been treated, Prospero, by an act of will, leashes his fury and allows his 'nobler reason' to dominate. An irrational abandonment to anger and to desire for revenge is replaced by a greater consciousness, an exercise of goodness towards the rest of humanity:

> The rarer action is
> In virtue than in vengeance.

(V.1.27–28)

How quietly is this profound moral recognition uttered!

The exercise of this 'virtue' — this vision of a felt human response replacing that of the magician, manipulator and controller — has deep implications for Prospero's inner life and for his dealings with others. In a long and powerful soliloquy (V.1.33–57) he establishes a new view of himself. First he summons all the spirits of nature that he has learnt to control: 'Ye elves of hills, brooks, standing lakes, and groves/ . . . you demi-puppets . . ./ . . . you whose pastime/ Is to make midnight mushrumps' (V.1.33–39). We glimpse his intimate penetration of all aspects of the natural world with, in the first ten lines or so, a relishing of its secret and fugitive qualities. What is more delicate and delightful than the notion of elves that play on the exposed sands between incoming waves without for a second imprinting themselves on the beach? But what at first appears to be a summons to these, his servants, turns into an assertion of personal power:

> . . . to the dread rattling thunder

> Have I given fire, and rifted Jove's stout oak
> With his own bolt; the strong-based promontory
> Have I made shake . . .

> (V.1.44–47)

Prospero has played God and, as the speech develops, an expanding sequence of boasting assertions — which includes this mastery over the elements, this shaking of the earth and violation of old and great trees, the very symbols of life — leads on to the most frightening boast of all:

> . . . graves at my command
> Have waked their sleepers, oped, and let them forth
> By my so potent art.

> (V.1.48–50)

It is a blatant assumption of divine power, a meddling with life and death. But there is no doubt about Prospero's boast: he is increasingly caught up in a sort of inflated admiration for his own powers as if he must relish and possess them to the uttermost before he will lay them down. That final phrase, 'By my so potent art', is a mere redundancy, a repetition of what he has already said, but it becomes a climactic, triumphant claim.

But that is not where the matter rests, for Prospero, as we have seen, has recognised his oneness with all of struggling humanity and can no longer lead the life of a remote and distanced magician. In another of those remarkable switches of mood that we have come to associate with him, his tone changes and the note of renunciation, the beginning of humility, is sounded:

> But this rough magic
> I here abjure, and when I have required
> Some heavenly music . . .
> . . . I'll break my staff,
> Bury it certain fathoms in the earth

> (V.1.50–55)

This is the vital transformation, the start of a new inner life in which Prospero, acknowledging his creaturely condition, is enabled to enter into relationship with his friends. He greets Gonzalo as his wise and venerated mentor. He rejoices in the new love of Ferdinand and Miranda and shares it with Alonso. He forgives his enemies, accepting the presence of malicious evil in the persons of Antonio and Sebastian as something that must be lived with and controlled. He knows now that the bestiality of Caliban is a part of himself for which he must take responsibility. He restores freedom to Ariel, that imaginative faculty necessarily shackled and kept within bounds to create this new world of human interaction. And, finally, as he resumes his duties as a ruler in the world of men, he knows himself to be a man subject to the limitations of our lives. Instead of the magician asserting power over life and death, he will:

> ... thence retire me to my Milan, where
> Every third thought shall be my grave.

(V.1.311–312)

AFTERTHOUGHTS

1

Wilson describes Prospero at one point as 'schoolmasterly' (page 103). What do you take this to mean? How apt do you find it?

2

Explain the point of Wilson's references to the Bible on page 104 and the importance of Christian thought to his argument as a whole.

3

How sympathetic a view of Caliban is put forward in this essay?

4

How significant is the idea of change to *The Tempest* as a whole?

Charles Moseley

Charles Moseley teaches English at Cambridge University and at the Leys School, Cambridge. He is the author of numerous critical studies.

ESSAY

Masque spectacle in *The Tempest*

Whatever else it is — and it is a lot else — *The Tempest* is at least in some measure 'about' illusion. And illusion lies at the root of the relationship between the real world and the theatre that is one of the ways of interpreting it. No other play of Shakespeare's so persistently draws attention to itself as a play. I am thinking not only of the celebrated ambiguity of the Epilogue, where Prospero might or might not be speaking in the person of the author thinking of his art of illusion, but also of the way we are constantly reminded that what characters in the play have no choice but to see as real is in fact stage-managed by Prospero. The whole of I.2, for instance, serves as a sort of explicatory Induction, such as might preface a masque, to a drama that demonstrates a moment of transformation and fruition where we need to know more than any character within the action. Moreover, the trick of illusion is played not only on characters within the play but on the audience too: the first scene looks and feels real when we first watch it, and there is no doubt that Alonso and his companions get a fair wetting; yet almost immediately Prospero reassures Miranda and ourselves that what we have seen is in fact an illusion contained and controlled within an as yet undiscovered higher purpose. Here I shall examine two scenes, III.3 and IV.1, where this sort of problem is particularly acute. In them Shakespeare draws heavily on the conventions and expectations of masque, and discussion of these elements will involve some consideration of what Prospero's purpose is, and relate to a central idea of the play, the relationship between 'nature' and 'nurture'.

It is all very well to use the word 'masque' to signify merely deliberately unrealistic and symbolic, even what we might call pantomime, elements in the play. But Renaissance masques could be much more serious and subtle than such a summary might suggest. Some are utterly trivial; but some of the best minds of Shakespeare's day and later — Ben Jonson, for example, or Milton — worked in masque with a high seriousness, and the exploitation of music and elaborate scenery as well as verse not only suggests the amount of hard cash people were prepared to spend on it — a measure of its recognised importance in itself — but also indicates its place in the ancestry of the important later form of opera.

The masque in the early seventeenth century is exclusively a court entertainment, lavish in production: Charles I is known to have spent over £20,000 on some single performances. They were often topical, designed for one specific occasion, public or private: Prospero's marriage masque would lose all relevance once Ferdinand and Miranda are married. The illusion of the masque often embraces the real role of one or more of the people within it or in its audience — James I as a watching king round whom the masque focuses, for example. The audience is expected to have some knowledge of classical mythology, and some understanding of music and dancing as highly intellectual ways of symbolising and defining a relationship between man's life on earth and the harmonious regimen of the ordered heavens above. It also demanded a familiarity with that language of visual and verbal symbol which formed an essential part of public and political life, and which was the recognised Renaissance way of making it possible to explore abstract ideas that could not be discussed easily or decorously in any other way — a means of saying the unsayable. In the best masques, watching it or acting in it is intended to affect the real lives men and women lead, just as Prospero presents an ideal of Good

Marriage in the masque he stages for the betrothal of Ferdinand and Miranda.

The use of masque in *The Tempest*, therefore, is more than just a way of separating the illusions *within* the play from the illusion of the whole; it alerts us to the importance of the generalised and abstract ideas that lie behind its immediate fable, and underlines that the whole play is an illusion whose meaning, like that of the real world, is not obvious. The art of Prospero, and of the dramatist whom he figures, is derivative from and symbolic of the Art of God who created the world we have to interpret.

Prospero, whose name is as openly symbolic as Miranda's,[1] manipulates the entire action. He is much more than just a wizard; in I.2 it is revealed that he is magus, learned in the high art of *magia* which Renaissance men took entirely seriously. His control of spirits is something real men sought — the power of harnessing good spirits to the restoration of the world's pristine perfection, the art of theurgy (as distinct from 'goety', using bad spirits, which we might call black magic.) That Prospero has this power would for a Renaissance audience be proof enough of his moral goodness. But in seeking it Duke Prospero had neglected the public duties of his role, and had been the victim of an intrigue he could not control. Now, having achieved a mastery over himself symbolised by his mastery over the island and its spirits, and acknowledging that within himself there are things of darkness, an impulsive nature, control of which is essential to true nobility (cf. V.1.275–276), he can repair the damages in the dark backward and abysm of time in a future where men of sin are brought to a knowledge of themselves. The new-found harmony can be expressed in a marriage that finally reconciles two antagonistic royal houses. That marriage is more than a neat political solution, for in *magia*, a central principle is the notion of gender in all things, from chemical elements to

---

[1] *Miranda* = 'to be admired or wondered at' — almost 'a marvel'. Cf. III.1.37–38, where Shakespeare uses Ferdinand to make this explicit. Prospero (*pro + spero*) may be interpreted as 'I hope for the future' — and Prospero's thought, even his third one, is all for the future's healing of past strife. Caliban is an anagram of 'canibal' — the savages Shakespeare read about in Florio's translation of Montaigne's essay 'Of the Canniballes'.

spirits; harmony, perfection and stability is achieved through marriage, the balancing of masculine and feminine in a new whole. Prospero's manipulation, therefore, is a means to the achievement of a proper moral and political balance between, on the one hand, human impulse and will — nature — and, on the other, the intellect that must rule this little kingdom of man — nurture.

His main means of manipulation is the creation of illusion which the viewers in the play experience as a reality they cannot control or understand. But we, sharing (after I.2) the perspective of Prospero, understand more than any other character, and therefore are aware of some larger design into which their experience is being composed. In I.2 Ferdinand is led to Miranda by the song Prospero made Ariel sing. Each at first sees the other as 'spirit' or 'goddess' rather than human, unsure whether what they see is on the same plane of being as themselves. Finding that they are, the first part of Prospero's design — their falling in love — is achieved. In II.1, we get our first full view of 'civilised' men, where we see both good — Gonzalo — and evil — Sebastian and Antonio, who want to make the tragic history of deposition and revolt repeat itself. The second part of Prospero's design is to purge this earlier evil and to preserve the true king. Alonso and Gonzalo are protected by Prospero's sending the invisible Ariel to wake them with music. This sort of manipulation is never far away in the play, and it is important to recognise that major structural plot devices are advanced by explicitly non-naturalistic means. But the concerns these scenes hint at are much more openly presented in the two most obvious 'masque scenes': III.3, the banquet, and IV.1, the marriage masque.

Act III, scene 3 falls into three parts, divided by the three spectacles managed by Ariel, and works on two levels: the spectacle and its symbolism, and the response of Alonso's company to it. Thus, part of the scene's interest lies in watching people respond to illusion — a self-reference typical of the play. Even though the masque elements are not as concentrated as they are in IV.1, the staging is elaborate, clearly demanding complex scenery, machinery and visual effects. We know that the play was produced at court in 1611, and at the Blackfriars Theatre as well as (probably) at the Globe. In at least the first two places elaborate staging was customary and indeed expected, and this scene, the most visually elaborate in Shakespeare's work, would have presented few difficulties. It opens, quite naturalistically, with the company divided into two moral groupings that echo what has been revealed in II.1 — Alonso with Gonzalo, Sebastian plotting murder with Antonio. Then, to the accompaniment of the 'solemn and strange music', symbolising a harmony the scene's first lines do *not* show in human affairs and signalling the importance of what is to come, the human characters are upstaged for several minutes by the 'strange shapes' setting a table, laying out the 'banquet' (i.e. delicate meats and sweetmeats taken after the main meal) and dancing their invitation to eat. The relation between the watchers and this action is exactly that between an audience and a masque; indeed, it would not be difficult to find in the records of Renaissance ceremonial, examples of invitations to formal feasts, in exactly this mode. But it is given an ironic twist by the audience watching the watchers being taken in by the illusion of Prospero, who suddenly enters above, on a level that symbolises his overall control and capacity to test and judge. Prospero as impresario, so to speak, comments as a chorus on the reactions of the King's party to what they have seen; and those reactions to the masque show that it has challenged them to understand what they are.

The symbolism of eating is fundamental. Alonso and his company are, it seems to him at least (cf. the hint in line 21), offered, by grace, heavenly food. The links to the Mass are clear. Eating this heavenly food in company is not only a symbol of harmony and communion but also of worthiness to partake. But Antonio and Sebastian react merely with scornful flippancy: Sebastian in lines 41ff shows himself as a clumsy sensualist — food is merely food, and has no further significance. He laughs at grace, and Antonio turns the miracle into a cheap joke about traveller's tales. Neither sees beyond the mere appearance. Gonzalo, on the other hand, recognises with awe that the strangeness of the figures who served the food was accompanied by indications of a moral goodness rare among human beings: the strange forces judgement of the familiar. Alonso recognises his own unworthiness to taste it. It is when he overcomes this misgiving, and he, Sebastian and Antonio presume to eat, that the banquet disappears in an antithesis of music, the noises of storm symbolic of disruption in microcosm and macrocosm.

Again, this moment is elaborately staged. The stage direction (line 52) is very close to Virgil's *Aeneid* III.225–228. Ariel's appearance '*like a harpy*' (the clever illusion of which Prospero later — lines 84–85 — emphasises) directly borrows from Virgil, who describes the harpies as birds with the faces of women, pallid with hunger; their hands are crooked claws, and their bellies emit filthy excrement. In the Renaissance they were supposed to be agents of divine vengeance, and clearly this is part of Prospero's symbolism, and part of Gonzalo's and Alonso's understanding. But the Virgilian link is yet closer: Aeneas and his companions land on the Strophades after a long, storm-tossed journey seeking their promised land. Killing the wild cattle they find there, they prepare a meal, only to have it twice ruined by the harpies. Then, fruitlessly, they take up arms to defend themselves against them, but can harm no feather of them. Celaeno, the leading harpy, reproves them for their foolishness in attacking them, and promises that they will come to their destined Italy only after more suffering and hunger.

An age that knew its Virgil very well indeed, and often read the *Aeneid* as symbolic of man's moral progress through the storms of life to the recognition of his true good, could hardly not spot the parallel with Alonso and his company: voyaging from the Tunis that Gonzalo identifies with the Carthage of Dido, where Aeneas underwent a temptation that nearly deflected him from his destiny, to their home in Italy, they are 'wrecked', cast ashore in an isle full of noises, and their hunger is baulked of satisfaction by the appearance of a 'harpy', against whom they take up fruitless arms, who reminds them of their guilt and promises them hardship and remorse. The parallel suggests to us a way of seeing how Prospero interprets their voyage and what he is doing to them; if they are all as fond of Virgil as Gonzalo is (II.1.76ff), it suggests a way the wiser in the company may interpret what they have just suffered.

The elaborate visual effect, therefore, helps to focus the meaning of the scene. In the disruption of the banquet there is also the obviously symbolic (as in *Macbeth*) destruction of a feast, commonly an expression of community and political harmony. The advantage of using masque techniques is obvious: it allows Shakespeare to introduce three visual spectacles with overt symbolism that can be directly, explicitly and decorously applied to the action they interrupt; it allows him to move into a non-naturalistic mode of signifying complex moral issues which the normal action of a play, which at least on the surface has to remain naturalistic, would not allow. It forces us to watch the reactions and interpretations of the watchers; and by keeping Prospero as impresario visible throughout, Shakespeare can remind us not only of Prospero's control of an illusion that others can only perceive as experienced reality, but also of his relationship to the playwright who is creating the total illusion for us. The scene contains within itself a little masque, and as a whole its subject is the watching of and reaction to the masque. The stately opening gives way to the 'anti-masque' ugliness[2] of Ariel's appearance. After both, its audience's reaction is central to our interest; and after a clap of thunder, recalling the thunder through which Jove spoke, Ariel vanishes and the spirits return to remove the table, with soft music and dancing. The scene's conclusion is the self-recognition of Alonso, without which he cannot go on to reconciliation with Prospero, and the folly of Sebastian and Antonio, whose nurture does not prevent their nature going bad. What tests one man and leads him to growth pushes two others towards a moral self-destruction worse than any ignorance of Caliban's.

The following scene, IV.1, divides into two halves: the marriage masque, and the foiling of the conspiracy of Trinculo, Stephano and Caliban. Lines 1–31 are occupied with Prospero bestowing Miranda on Ferdinand, with the strictest injunctions to follow virtue and not allow baser nature to overcome moral restraint. The ideas of fruitful and unfruitful agriculture in lines 13ff are closely linked to the images of fruitfulness and plenty in the masque that follows. That masque is, in fact, an elaborate way for Prospero to pronounce his blessing on the couple.

Prospero has evidently promised to show 'some vanity of

---

[2] Masques frequently included anti-masques — comic or ugly moments, with appropriately discordant music, symbolising the containment of dangerous disorder within order.

mine Art'[3] to them, and they are given a celebratory masque exactly like those composed to honour such real occasions as royal marriages or engagements. It is prefaced by a command for the silence (line 59; repeated at lines 126–127) essential to acts of *magia*; this underlines the importance Prospero attaches to what he has devised. The masque is his way of saying the unsayable, of expressing through elaborate symbol and metaphor both the depth of his love for Miranda and his hopes for the future of the pair who, as rulers, will be responsible for the husbandry of their realms. The masque thus indicates that a central interest in the play, the resolution of which is utterly dependent on this marriage, is the proper ruling both of natural desires by intellect and of the kingdom by virtue.

The symbol of Iris, messenger of the gods, is the rainbow (line 71), sign of a covenant between God and man. Her verse, like that of the masque generally, sounds a new note in the play: it is noticeably stiffer, more ceremonious, more formal and elaborately rhetorical than elsewhere — a rhetorical mode typical of pageant verse. Iris' decasyllabic couplets are structured into an elaborate apostrophe whose sense is not completed until the commands to Ceres of lines 70–74; the language bombards us with ideas of agricultural plenty appropriate to Ceres' patronage of crops and flocks. Iris' closing lines are accompanied by the *coup de théâtre* of the descent of Juno, queen of the gods and patroness of marriage, from the heavens (theatrical and cosmic) to take her part in this masque of blessing.[4]

As she asks why she has been summoned, Ceres returns with interest Iris' ideas of fruitfulness and the richness of the earth's bounty. But when asked to celebrate this 'contract of true love', she is careful first to enquire whether Venus, goddess of love is present. Ceres' old enmity to Venus sprang from the

---

[3] The word 'vanity' perhaps anticipates his later rejection of his 'rough magic'. His readiness to *use* this art is coupled with the recognition that its mastery is only an interim stage on the way to his ultimate goal, moral perfection.

[4] The 'peacocks' of line 74 probably were represented — possibly by stuffed specimens. Juno's peacock-drawn chariot is so standard a feature of her appearances that it can hardly have been left out. In *Cymbeline* V.4, Jupiter descends from the heavens on an eagle.

fact that Venus had made Dis (Pluto), god of the underworld, fall in love with and ravish her daughter Proserpine. Proserpine's departure from the earth for Hades caused unfruitfulness and dearth, and only when she returned for her visit each spring to the upper world did the earth bloom again. The inclusion of this idea is significant; for Caliban, a thing of darkness, had attempted or desired of Miranda the thing that 'dusky Dis' had achieved, and it is specifically against giving rein to such sexual desire that Prospero warns Ferdinand. Such love has to be sublimated to a higher, intellectual, love before it can be used properly: otherwise it blasts with sterility. (This is perfectly sensible Renaissance moral philosophy.) So Iris reassures Ceres that though indeed there was temptation between the lovers, Venus and Cupid have gone (lines 94ff): Ferdinand and Miranda have mastered their desires. Prospero is reinforcing the point made earlier, that innocence is good in itself, but virtue is the fruit only of that innocence being tested.

Juno and Ceres now move into songs of blessing: twelve lines of octosyllabic couplets promising personal happiness to the couple and prosperity to their land. In them the Golden Age is glimpsed again, but the precariousness of this vision is delicately hinted by Juno and Ceres using verbs not in the future indicative but in the optative subjunctive mood. These are not predictions but wishes, dependent on the conduct of Ferdinand and Miranda. Thus the masque is being used once again, as so commonly, both as interpretation and as injunction. Prospero is reinforcing the direct lesson of lines 1–30 by something imaginatively much more gripping, memorable and fruitful because of its ambiguity.

We may, I think, be sure that this is why Ferdinand interrupts at line 118. The next ten lines shift the focus back from what we are watching *with* Ferdinand and Prospero to watching how Ferdinand reacts. The dramatic texture becomes more subtle by this, for we are reminded, as Prospero reminds Ferdinand, that it is not goddesses but Prospero's servant spirits who perform his masque of blessing. It is not the blessing directly of heaven. Yet, as Ferdinand's reference to Paradise (line 124) hints, he seems to have recognised in Prospero the type of the philosopher king, who by his virtue and wisdom is nearest the gods. Thus in a sense Prospero's blessing is the blessing of heaven, which must be taken out of the enchanted island and put to work.

That Ferdinand and Miranda will be able to do this is, I think, indicated by what happens when Prospero suddenly ends the masque: at line 164 they leave him, and go into his cell, and the next time we see them they form the climatic tableau that resolves the entire play, when Prospero is known for what he is, when Alonso has his son restored, and when the political wrongs are righted. When Prospero draws the curtain on them, they are discovered playing the noblest of games, chess, a game which for centuries had symbolised the love-battle, where yielding and victory are meaningless terms because each depends on the other, and where impulse is subject to rigid rules.

After the blessing Iris summons chaste ('temperate') nymphs, the Naiads, to dance with the harvestmen to celebrate these nuptials: in the graceful dance, image of order, the plenty of harvest and the heat of summer harmoniously combine with the cool moisture that makes the fields fruitful. In this dance, watched by Juno, Ceres and Iris, there is an increasingly confident foreshadowing of joy. But in the very moment of its execution, Prospero's memory suddenly recalls the planned rebellion of Caliban: and the masque ends in confusion. Just so would the rebellion of the baser nature wreck the harmony of a marriage of true minds.

It is clear what sort of masque it is that Shakespeare has given Prospero: it is to serve as a prothalamion, a celebration of the coming marriage, a proclamation of its ideals, and an emphasis of its preciousness. Its interruption, however, complicates the issue somewhat, for it recalls that despite this harmony there is still discord in the island. This scene as a whole has two main divisions: the troth-plighting, projected allegorically into a future that, given purity, will be fruitful, and the impure conspiracy to seize power of Stephano and Trinculo, unable to rule themselves, with Caliban who attempted to ravish Miranda. These two areas meet in Prospero's mind. But those who served in the masque are now turned against the confederacy of the impure, and at the end, in a sort of knock-about anti-masque, Stephano and Trinculo take all appearance for reality until finally they are hunted by their own base desires, given appropriate physical form.

Those animal desires remind us that underlying the entire play and its examination of how people respond to experience and the challenge of illusion is the idea of man as a thinking *animal*, distinguished from the brutes only by Reason. The danger of him regressing into animality is ever present, and the civilised man who goes savage is worse than the savage who never was anything else: Stephano and Trinculo are far more repulsive than Caliban, and Antonio and Sebastian have even less excuse for their evil. Caliban, a stage-figure straight from the masque tradition of the wild man, shows the deeper corruption of the civilised when they go bad; yet he himself is dangerous, like Spenser's Salvage Man in *The Faerie Queene* — instinctively helpful, but also liable to give way to his untrained and animal impulses in rape and violence.

Prospero knows that to avoid disaster the lower human nature must be ruled by Reason and Art. He knows that just as true marriage must reconcile masculine and feminine principles, and balance the desire to procreate and the desire to restrain, so the wise and virtuous man, the philosopher king, has to balance his higher and his lower nature. He has to acknowledge the Caliban in himself: he has to recognise his own mortality, reject the rough magic that has been only the means to beginning the search for true wisdom, and give a third of his thought to his grave. And the philosopher has a responsibility to educate, to pass on his wisdom.

The play quite openly concerns itself with education. Prospero teaches Miranda and Ferdinand the importance of self-rule both directly and through his stage-managing of what they perceive; they have to recognise that it is their job to control the evil in their world. Alonso is educated into repentance and reconciliation. Miranda's holy and pure natural instincts need* educating to the recognition that by that very fact she is vulnerable to the attack of Caliban, to the deceit of that fair-seeming brave new world which contains that which would destroy her innocence, and to the fire in the blood she little suspects in herself. Her impulse to educate is part of her nobility, but as yet she is unable to master Caliban on whose nature no print of nurture will ever stick. She has to be taught a wisdom and discrimination that Prospero learnt by suffering.

Yet, while the central antithesis in the play is between

nature and the art of understanding life which is summed up in the word nurture, it will not reduce itself to simple formulas and easy answers. Just as Ferdinand glimpsed through Prospero's masque a truth inexhaustible and not reducible to precept, so we watching the play have been through an experience that in occupying real time has changed us irrevocably in a way that is not readily amenable to summary. Within the play the two masques operate as expressions of a complex moral reality; watching people within the play experience illusion makes us examine our response to the illusion of the whole, and its relevance and importance in what Sir Walter Ralegh called 'this stage play world' in which we live.

AFTERTHOUGHTS

1

Compare Moseley's opening comments about 'illusion' with Peter Reynolds's comments in the first essay (pages 9–18). What views of 'illusion' are being expressed?

2

Before you read this essay, what did you take to be the 'overt symbolism' (page 120) of the masque?

3

How helpful do you find Moseley's account of *magia* (pages 116–117)?

4

Why does Moseley highlight the links between *The Tempest* and Virgil's *Aeneid* (page 119)?

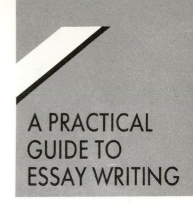

A PRACTICAL GUIDE TO ESSAY WRITING

INTRODUCTION

First, a word of warning. Good essays are the product of a creative engagement with literature. So never try to restrict your studies to what you think will be 'useful in the exam'. Ironically, you will restrict your grade potential if you do.

This doesn't mean, of course, that you should ignore the basic skills of essay writing. When you read critics, make a conscious effort to notice *how* they communicate their ideas. The guidelines that follow offer advice of a more explicit kind. But they are no substitute for practical experience. It is never easy to express ideas with clarity and precision. But the more often you tackle the problems involved and experiment to find your own voice, the more fluent you will become. So practise writing essays as often as possible.

HOW TO PLAN AN ESSAY

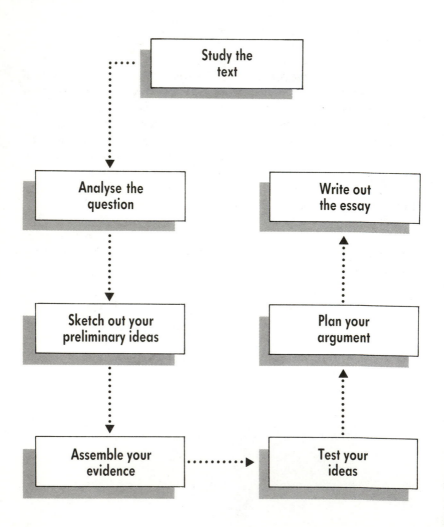

Study the text

The first step in writing a good essay is to get to know the set text well. Never write about a text until you are fully familiar with it. Even a discussion of the opening chapter of a novel, for example, should be informed by an understanding of the book as a whole. Literary texts, however, are by their very nature complex and on a first reading you are bound to miss many significant features. Re-read the book with care, if possible more than once. Look up any unfamiliar words in a good dictionary and if the text you are studying was written more than a few decades ago, consult the *Oxford English Dictionary* to find out whether the meanings of any terms have shifted in the intervening period.

Good books are difficult to put down when you first read them. But a more leisurely second or third reading gives you the opportunity to make notes on those features you find significant. An index of characters and events is often useful, particularly when studying novels with a complex plot or time scheme. The main aim, however, should be to record your *responses* to the text. By all means note, for example, striking images. But be sure to add *why* you think them striking. Similarly, record any thoughts you may have on interesting comparisons with other texts, puzzling points of characterisation, even what you take to be aesthetic blemishes. The important thing is to annotate fully and adventurously. The most seemingly idiosyncratic comment may later lead to a crucial area of discussion which you would otherwise have overlooked. It helps to have a working copy of the text in which to mark up key passages and jot down marginal comments (although obviously these practices are taboo when working with library, borrowed or valuable copies!). But keep a fuller set of notes as well and organise these under appropriate headings.

Literature does not exist in an aesthetic vacuum, however, and you should try to find out as much as possible about the context of its production and reception. It is particularly important to read other works by the same author and writings by contemporaries. At this early stage, you may want to restrict your secondary reading to those standard reference works, such as biographies, which are widely available in public libraries. In the long run, however, it pays to read as wide a range of critical studies as possible.

Some students, and tutors, worry that such studies may stifle the development of any truly personal response. But this won't happen if you are alert to the danger and read critically. After all, you wouldn't passively accept what a stranger told you in conversation. The fact that a critic's views are in print does not necessarily make them any more authoritative (as a glance at the review pages of the *TLS* and *London Review of Books* will reveal). So question the views you find: 'Does this critic's interpretation agree with mine and where do we part company?' 'Can it be right to try and restrict this text's meanings to those found by its author or first audience?' 'Doesn't this passage treat a theatrical text as though it were a novel?' Often it is views which you reject which prove most valuable since they challenge you to articulate your own position with greater clarity. Be sure to keep careful notes on what the critic wrote, and your *reactions* to what the critic wrote.

Analyse the question

You cannot begin to answer a question until you understand what task it is you have been asked to perform. Recast the question in your own words and reconstruct the line of reasoning which lies behind it. Where there is a choice of topics, try to choose the one for which you are best prepared. It would, for example, be unwise to tackle 'How far do you agree that in *Paradise Lost* Milton transformed the epic models he inherited from ancient Greece and Rome?' without a working knowledge of Homer and Virgil (or *Paradise Lost* for that matter!). If you do not already know the works of these authors, the question should spur you on to read more widely — or discourage you from attempting it at all. The scope of an essay, however, is not always so obvious and you must remain alert to the implied demands of each question. How could you possibly 'Consider the view that *Wuthering Heights* transcends the conventions of the Gothic novel' without reference to at least some of those works which, the question suggests, have *not* transcended Gothic conventions?

When you have decided on a topic, analyse the terms of the question itself. Sometimes these self-evidently require careful definition: *tragedy* and *irony*, for example, are notoriously difficult concepts to pin down and you will probably need to consult a good dictionary of literary terms. Don't ignore, however, those seemingly innocuous phrases which often smuggle in significant assumptions. 'Does Macbeth lack the nobility of the true tragic hero?' obviously invites you to discuss nobility and the nature of the tragic hero. But what of 'lack' and 'true' — do they suggest that the play would be improved had Shakespeare depicted Macbeth in a different manner? or that tragedy is superior to other forms of drama? Remember that you are not expected meekly to agree with the assumptions implicit in the question. Some questions are deliberately provocative in order to stimulate an engaged response. Don't be afraid to take up the challenge.

Sketch out your preliminary ideas

'Which comes first, the evidence or the answer?' is one of those chicken and egg questions. How can you form a view without inspecting the evidence? But how can you know which evidence is relevant without some idea of what it is you are looking for? In practice the mind reviews evidence and formulates preliminary theories or hypotheses at one and the same time, although for the sake of clarity we have separated out the processes. Remember that these early ideas are only there to get you started. You *expect* to modify them in the light of the evidence you uncover. Your initial hypothesis may be an instinctive 'gut-reaction'. Or you may find that you prefer to 'sleep on the problem', allowing ideas to gell over a period of time. Don't worry in either case. The mind is quite capable of processing a vast amount of accumulated evidence, the product of previous reading and thought, and reaching sophisticated intuitive judgements. Eventually, however, you are going to have to think carefully through any ideas you arrive at by such intuitive processes. Are they logical? Do they take account of all the relevant factors? Do they fully answer the question set? Are there any obvious reasons to qualify or abandon them?

Assemble your evidence

Now is the time to return to the text and re-read it with the question and your working hypothesis firmly in mind. Many of the notes you have already made are likely to be useful, but assess the precise relevance of this material and make notes on any new evidence you discover. The important thing is to cast your net widely and take into account points which tend to undermine your case as well as those that support it. As always, ensure that your notes are full, accurate, and reflect your own critical judgements.

You may well need to go outside the text if you are to do full justice to the question. If you think that the 'Oedipus complex' may be relevant to an answer on *Hamlet* then read Freud and a balanced selection of those critics who have discussed the appropriateness of applying psychoanalytical theories to the interpretation of literature. Their views can most easily be tracked down by consulting the annotated bibliographies held by most major libraries (and don't be afraid to ask a librarian for help in finding and using these). Remember that you go to works of criticism not only to obtain information but to stimulate you into clarifying your own position. And that since life is short and many critical studies are long, judicious use of a book's index and/or contents list is not to be scorned. You can save yourself a great deal of future labour if you carefully record full bibliographic details at this stage.

Once you have collected the evidence, organise it coherently. Sort the detailed points into related groups and identify the quotations which support these. You must also assess the relative importance of each point, for in an essay of limited length it is essential to establish a firm set of priorities, exploring some ideas in depth while discarding or subordinating others.

Test your ideas

As we stressed earlier, a hypothesis is only a proposal, and one that you fully expect to modify. Review it with the evidence before you. Do you really still believe in it? It would be surprising if you did not want to modify it in some way. If you cannot see any problems, others may. Try discussing your ideas with friends and relatives. Raise them in class discussions. Your tutor is certain to welcome your initiative. The critical process is essentially collaborative and there is absolutely no reason why you should not listen to and benefit from the views of others. Similarly, you should feel free to test your ideas against the theories put forward in academic journals and books. But do not just borrow what you find. Critically analyse the views on offer and, where appropriate, integrate them into your own pattern of thought. You must, of course, give full acknowledgement to the sources of such views.

Do not despair if you find you have to abandon or modify significantly your initial position. The fact that you are prepared to do so is a mark of intellectual integrity. Dogmatism is never an academic virtue and many of the best essays explore the *process* of scholarly enquiry rather than simply record its results.

Plan your argument

Once you have more or less decided on your attitude to the question (for an answer is never really 'finalised') you have to present your case in the most persuasive manner. In order to do this you must avoid meandering from point to point and instead produce an organised argument — a structured flow of ideas and supporting evidence, leading logically to a conclusion which fully answers the question. Never begin to write until you have produced an outline of your argument.

You may find it easiest to begin by sketching out its main stage as a flow chart or some other form of visual presentation. But eventually you should produce a list of paragraph topics. The paragraph is the conventional written demarcation for a unit of thought and you can outline an argument quite simply by briefly summarising the substance of each paragraph and then checking that these points (you may remember your English teacher referring to them as topic sentences) really do follow a coherent order. Later you will be able to elaborate on each topic, illustrating and qualifying it as you go along. But you will find this far easier to do if you possess from the outset a clear map of where you are heading.

All questions require some form of an argument. Even so-called 'descriptive' questions *imply* the need for an argument. An adequate answer to the request to 'Outline the role of Iago in *Othello*' would do far more than simply list his appearances on stage. It would at the very least attempt to provide some *explanation* for his actions — is he, for example, a representative stage 'Machiavel'? an example of pure evil, 'motiveless malignity'? or a realistic study of a tormented personality reacting to identifiable social and psychological pressures?

Your conclusion ought to address the terms of the question. It may seem obvious, but 'how far do you agree', 'evaluate', 'consider', 'discuss', etc, are *not* interchangeable formulas and your conclusion must take account of the precise wording of the question. If asked 'How far do you agree?', the concluding paragraph of your essay really should state whether you are in complete agreement, total disagreement, or, more likely, partial agreement. Each preceding paragraph should have a clear justification for its existence and help to clarify the reasoning which underlies your conclusion. If you find that a paragraph serves no good purpose (perhaps merely summarising the plot), do not hesitate to discard it.

The arrangement of the paragraphs, the overall strategy of the argument, can vary. One possible pattern is dialectical: present the arguments in favour of one point of view (**thesis**); then turn to counter-arguments or to a rival interpretation (**antithesis**); finally evaluate the competing claims and arrive at your own conclusion (**synthesis**). You may, on the other hand, feel so convinced of the merits of one particular case that you wish to devote your entire essay to arguing that viewpoint persuasively (although it is always desirable to indicate, however briefly, that you are aware of alternative, if flawed, positions). As the essays contained in this volume demonstrate, there are many other possible strategies. Try to adopt the one which will most comfortably accommodate the demands of the question and allow you to express your thoughts with the greatest possible clarity.

Be careful, however, not to apply abstract formulas in a mechanical manner. It is true that you should be careful to define your terms. It is *not* true that every essay should begin with 'The dictionary defines *x* as . . .'. In fact, definitions are often best left until an appropriate moment for their introduction arrives. Similarly every essay should have a beginning, middle and end. But it does not follow that in your opening paragraph you should announce an intention to write an essay, or that in your concluding paragraph you need to signal an imminent desire to put down your pen. The old adages are often useful reminders of what constitutes good practice, but they must be interpreted intelligently.

Write out the essay

Once you have developed a coherent argument you should aim to communicate it in the most effective manner possible. Make certain you clearly identify yourself, and the question you are answering. Ideally, type your answer, or at least ensure your handwriting is legible and that you leave sufficient space for your tutor's comments. Careless presentation merely distracts from the force of your argument. Errors of grammar, syntax and spelling are far more serious. At best they are an irritating blemish, particularly in the work of a student who should be sensitive to the nuances of language. At worst, they seriously confuse the sense of your argument. If you are aware that you have stylistic problems of this kind, ask your tutor for advice at the earliest opportunity. Everyone, however, is liable to commit the occasional howler. The only remedy is to give yourself plenty of time in which to proof-read your manuscript (often reading it aloud is helpful) before submitting it.

Language, however, is not only an instrument of communication; it is also an instrument of thought. If you want to think clearly and precisely you should strive for a clear, precise prose style. Keep your sentences short and direct. Use modern, straightforward English wherever possible. Avoid repetition, clichés and wordiness. Beware of generalisations, simplifications, and overstatements. Orwell analysed the relationship between stylistic vice and muddled thought in his essay 'Politics and the English Language' (1946) — it remains essential reading (and is still readily available in volume 4 of the Penguin *Collected Essays, Journalism and Letters*). Generalisations, for example, are always dangerous. They are rarely true and tend to suppress the individuality of the texts in question. A remark such as 'Keats always employs sensuous language in his poetry' is not only fatuous (what, after all, does it mean? is *every* word he wrote equally 'sensuous'?) but tends to obscure interesting distinctions which could otherwise be made between, say, the descriptions in the 'Ode on a Grecian Urn' and those in 'To Autumn'.

The intelligent use of quotations can help you make your points with greater clarity. Don't sprinkle them throughout your essay without good reason. There is no need, for example, to use them to support uncontentious statements of fact. 'Macbeth murdered Duncan' does not require textual evidence (unless you wish to dispute Thurber's brilliant parody, 'The Great Macbeth Murder Mystery', which reveals Lady Macbeth's father as the culprit!). Quotations should be included, however, when they are necessary to support your case. The proposition that Macbeth's imaginative powers wither after he has killed his king would certainly require extensive quotation: you would almost certainly want to analyse key passages from both before and after the murder (perhaps his first and last soliloquies?). The key word here is 'analyse'. Quotations cannot make your points on their own. It is up to you to demonstrate their relevance and clearly explain to your readers *why* you want them to focus on the passage you have selected.

Most of the academic conventions which govern the presentation of essays are set out briefly in the style sheet below. The question of gender, however, requires fuller discussion. More than half the population of the world is female. Yet many writers still refer to an undifferentiated *man*kind. Or write of the author and *his* public. We do not think that this convention has much to recommend it. At the very least, it runs the risk of introducing unintended sexist attitudes. And at times leads to such patent absurdities as 'Cleopatra's final speech asserts *man*'s true nobility'. With a little thought, you can normally find ways of expressing yourself which do not suggest that the typical author, critic or reader is male. Often you can simply use plural forms, which is probably a more elegant solution than relying on such awkward formulations as 's/he' or 'he and she'. You should also try to avoid distinguishing between male and female authors on the basis of forenames. Why *Jane* Austen and not *George* Byron? Refer to all authors by their last names unless there is some good reason not to. Where there may otherwise be confusion, say between T S and George Eliot, give the name in full when it first occurs and thereafter use the last name only.

Finally, keep your audience firmly in mind. Tutors and examiners are interested in understanding your conclusions and the processes by which you arrived at them. They are not interested in reading a potted version of a book they already know. **So don't pad out your work with plot summary.**

Hints for examinations

In an examination you should go through exactly the same processes as you would for the preparation of a term essay. The only difference lies in the fact that some of the stages will have had to take place before you enter the examination room. This should not bother you unduly. Examiners are bound to avoid the merely eccentric when they come to formulate papers and if you have read widely and thought deeply about the central issues raised by your set texts you can be confident you will have sufficient material to answer the majority of questions sensibly.

The fact that examinations impose strict time limits makes it *more* rather than less, important that you plan carefully. There really is no point in floundering into an answer without any idea of where you are going, particularly when there will not be time to recover from the initial error.

Before you begin to answer any question at all, study the entire paper with care. Check that you understand the rubric and know how many questions you have to answer and whether any are compulsory. It may be comforting to spot a title you feel confident of answering well, but don't rush to tackle it: read *all* the questions before deciding which *combination* will allow you to display your abilities to the fullest advantage. Once you have made your choice, analyse each question, sketch out your ideas, assemble the evidence, review your initial hypothesis, play your argument, *before* trying to write out an answer. And make notes at each stage: not only will these help you arrive at a sensible conclusion, but examiners are impressed by evidence of careful thought.

Plan your time as well as your answers. If you have practised writing timed essays as part of your revision, you should not find this too difficult. There can be a temptation to allocate extra time to the questions you know you can answer well; but this is always a short-sighted policy. You will find yourself left to face a question which would in any event have given you difficulty without even the time to give it serious thought. It is, moreover, easier to gain marks at the lower end of the scale than at the upper, and you will never compensate for one poor answer by further polishing two satisfactory answers. Try to leave some time at the end of the examination to re-read your answers and correct any obvious errors. If the worst comes to the worst and you run short of time, don't just keep writing until you are forced to break off in mid-paragraph. It is far better to provide for the examiner a set of notes which indicate the overall direction of your argument.

Good luck — but if you prepare for the examination conscientiously and tackle the paper in a methodical manner, you won't need it!

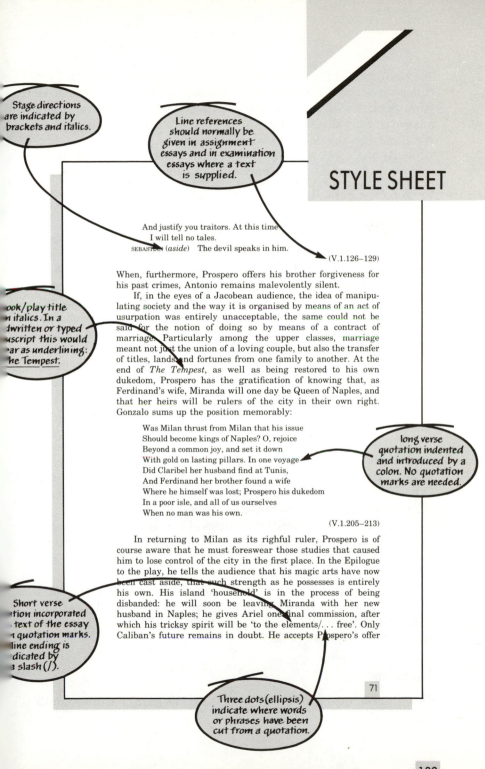

Stage directions are indicated by brackets and italics.

Line references should normally be given in assignment essays and in examination essays where a text is supplied.

And justify you traitors. At this time
I will tell no tales.
SEBASTIAN (*aside*)   The devil speaks in him.

(V.1.126–129)

When, furthermore, Prospero offers his brother forgiveness for his past crimes, Antonio remains malevolently silent.

If, in the eyes of a Jacobean audience, the idea of manipulating society and the way it is organised by means of an act of usurpation was entirely unacceptable, the same could not be said for the notion of doing so by means of a contract of marriage. Particularly among the upper classes, marriage meant not just the union of a loving couple, but also the transfer of titles, lands and fortunes from one family to another. At the end of *The Tempest*, as well as being restored to his own dukedom, Prospero has the gratification of knowing that, as Ferdinand's wife, Miranda will one day be Queen of Naples, and that her heirs will be rulers of the city in their own right. Gonzalo sums up the position memorably:

Book/play title in italics. In a handwritten or typed manuscript this would appear as underlining: The Tempest.

> Was Milan thrust from Milan that his issue
> Should become kings of Naples? O, rejoice
> Beyond a common joy, and set it down
> With gold on lasting pillars. In one voyage
> Did Claribel her husband find at Tunis,
> And Ferdinand her brother found a wife
> Where he himself was lost; Prospero his dukedom
> In a poor isle, and all of us ourselves
> When no man was his own.

(V.1.205–213)

Long verse quotation indented and introduced by a colon. No quotation marks are needed.

In returning to Milan as its righful ruler, Prospero is of course aware that he must foreswear those studies that caused him to lose control of the city in the first place. In the Epilogue to the play, he tells the audience that his magic arts have now been cast aside, that such strength as he possesses is entirely his own. His island 'household' is in the process of being disbanded: he will soon be leaving Miranda with her new husband in Naples; he gives Ariel one final commission, after which his tricksy spirit will be 'to the elements/. . . free'. Only Caliban's future remains in doubt. He accepts Prospero's offer

Short verse quotation incorporated in the text of the essay in quotation marks. A line ending is indicated by a slash (/).

Three dots (ellipsis) indicate where words or phrases have been cut from a quotation.

71

139

We have divided the following information into two sections. Part A describes those rules which it is essential to master no matter what kind of essay you are writing (including examination answers). Part B sets out some of the more detailed conventions which govern the documentation of essays.

PART A: LAYOUT

Titles of texts

Titles of published books, plays (of any length), long poems, pamphlets and periodicals (including newspapers and magazines), works of classical literature, and films should be underlined: e.g. David Copperfield (novel), Twelfth Night (play), Paradise Lost (long poem), Critical Quarterly (periodical), Horace's Ars Poetica (Classical work), Apocalypse Now (film).

Notice how important it is to distinguish between titles and other names. Hamlet is the play; Hamlet the prince. Wuthering Heights is the novel; Wuthering Heights the house. Underlining is the equivalent in handwritten or typed manuscripts of printed italics. So what normally appears in this volume as *Othello* would be written as Othello in your essay.

Titles of articles, essays, short stories, short poems, songs, chapters of books, speeches, and newspaper articles are enclosed in quotation marks; e.g. 'The Flea' (short poem), 'The Prussian Officer' (short story), 'Middleton's Chess Strategies' (article), 'Thatcher Defects!' (newspaper headline).

Exceptions: Underlining titles or placing them within quotation marks does not apply to sacred writings (e.g. Bible, Koran, Old Testament, Gospels) or parts of a book (e.g. Preface, Introduction, Appendix).

It is generally incorrect to place quotation marks around a title of a published book which you have underlined. The exception is 'titles within titles': e.g. 'Vanity Fair': A Critical Study (title of a book about *Vanity Fair*).

Quotations

Short verse quotations of a single line or part of a line should be incorporated within quotation marks as part of the running text of your essay. Quotations of two or three lines of verse are treated in the same way, with line endings indicated by a slash(/). For example:

1 In Julius Caesar, Antony says of Brutus, 'This was the noblest Roman of them all'.
2 The opening of Antony's famous funeral oration, 'Friends, Romans, Countrymen, lend me your ears;/ I come to bury Caesar not to praise him', is a carefully controlled piece of rhetoric.

Longer verse quotations of more than three lines should be indented from the main body of the text and introduced in most cases with a colon. Do not enclose indented quotations within quotation marks. For example:

It is worth pausing to consider the reasons Brutus gives to justify his decision to assassinate Caesar:

> It must be by his death; and for my part,
> I know no personal cause to spurn at him,
> But for the general. He would be crowned.
> How might that change his nature, there's the question.

At first glance his rationale may appear logical . . .

Prose quotations of less than three lines should be incorporated in the text of the essay, within quotation marks. Longer prose quotations should be indented and the quotation marks omitted. For example:

1 Before his downfall, Caesar rules with an iron hand. His political opponents, the Tribunes Marullus and Flavius, are 'put to silence' for the trivial offence of 'pulling scarfs off Caesar's image'.
2 It is interesting to note the rhetorical structure of Brutus's Forum speech:

> Romans, countrymen, and lovers, hear me for my cause, and be silent that you may hear. Believe me for my honour, and have respect to mine honour that you may believe. Censure me in your wisdom, and awake your senses, that you may the better judge.

Tenses: When you are relating the events that occur within a work of fiction, or describing the author's technique, it is the convention to use the present tense. Even though Orwell published *Animal Farm* in 1945, the book *describes* the animals' seizure of Manor Farm. Similarly, Macbeth always *murders* Duncan, despite the passage of time.

PART B: DOCUMENTATION

When quoting from verse of more than twenty lines, provide line references: e.g. In 'Upon Appleton House' Marvell's mower moves 'With whistling scythe and elbow strong' (1.393).

Quotations from plays should be identified by act, scene and line references: e.g. Prospero, in Shakespeare's The Tempest, refers to Caliban as 'A devil, a born devil' (IV.1.188). (i.e. Act 4. Scene 1. Line 188).

Quotations from prose works should provide a chapter reference and, where appropriate, a page reference.

Bibliographies should list full details of all sources consulted. The way is which they are presented varies, but one standard format is as follows:

1   Books and articles are listed in alphabetical order by the author's last name. Initials are placed after the surname.
2   If you are referring to a chapter or article within a larger work, you list it by reference to the author of the article or chapter, not the editor (although the editor is also named in the reference).
3   Give (in parentheses) the place and date of publication, e.g. (London, 1962). These details can be found within the book itself. Here are some examples:

> Brockbank, J. P., 'Shakespeare's Histories, English and Roman', in Ricks, C. (ed.) English Drama to 1710 (Sphere History of Literature in the English Language) (London, 1971).
> Gurr, A., 'Richard III and the Democratic Process', Essays in Criticism 24 (1974), pp. 39–47.
> Spivack, B., Shakespeare and the Allegory of Evil (New York, 1958).

Footnotes: In general, try to avoid using footnotes and build your references into the body of the essay wherever possible. When you do use them give the full bibliographic reference to a work in the first instance and then use a short title: e.g. See K. Smidt, <u>Unconformities in Shakespeare's History Plays</u> (London, 1982), pp. 43–47 becomes Smidt (pp. 43–47) thereafter. Do not use terms such as 'ibid.' or 'op. cit.' unless you are absolutely sure of their meaning.

There is a principle behind all this seeming pedantry. The reader ought to be able to find and check your references and quotations as quickly and easily as possible. Give additional information, such as canto or volume number whenever you think it will assist your reader.

SUGGESTIONS FOR FURTHER READING

Texts

The following editions offer particularly stimulating introductions:

Kermode, F (ed.), *The Tempest* (new Arden Shakespeare; London, 1954)

Righter, A (ed.), *The Tempest* (New Penguin Shakespeare; Harmondsworth, 1968)

Orgel, S (ed.), *The Tempest* (The Oxford Shakespeare; Oxford, 1987)

General studies (containing substantial discussions of *The Tempest*)

Brown, J R, and Harris, B (eds.), *Later Shakespeare* (Stratford-upon-Avon Studies 8; London, 1966)

Frye, N, *A Natural Perspective: The Development of Shakespearean Comedy and Romance* (New York, 1965)

Petersen, D, *Time, Tide and Tempest* (San Marino, 1973)

Wells, S (ed.), *The Cambridge Companion To Shakespeare* (Cambridge, 1986)

Studies of *The Tempest*

Brockbank, J P, '*The Tempest:* Conventions of Art and Empire', in Brown, J R, and Harris, B (eds), *Later Shakespeare* (Stratford-upon-Avon Studies 8; London, 1966)

Brown, P, '"This Thing of Darkness I Acknowledge Mine": *The Tempest* and the Discourse of Colonialism', in Dollimore, J, and Sinfield, A (eds), *Political Shakespeare* (London, 1985)

Clarke, S, *The Tempest* (Penguin Masterstudy; Harmondsworth, 1986)

Knox, B, '*The Tempest* and the Ancient Comic Tradition', in

Wimsatt, W K (ed.), *English Stage Comedy* (English Institute Essays, 1954; New York, 1955)

Loughrey, B, and Taylor, N, 'Ferdinand and Miranda at Chess', in *Shakespeare Survey* 35 (1982)

Zimbardo, R, 'Form and Disorder in *The Tempest*' in Palmer, D J (ed.), *Shakespeare's Later Comedies* (Penguin Shakespeare Library; Harmondsworth, 1971)

Robert Browning's 'Caliban Upon Setebos; or, Natural Theology in the Island' (1889) and W H Auden's 'The Sea and the Mirror' (1945) are major poetic achievements in their own right, but offer perceptive commentary on *The Tempest*.

Longman Group UK Limited
*Longman House, Burnt Mill, Harlow, Essex, CM20 2JE, England
and Associated Companies throughout the World.*

First published 1988
ISBN 0 582 00651 1

*Set in 10/12 pt Century Schoolbook, Linotron 202
Printed in Great Britain by Bell and Bain Ltd., Glasgow*

Acknowledgement
The editors would like to thank Zachary Leader for his assistance with the style sheet.